D1558221

A Theory of Language and Mind

A Theory of
Language and
Mind

Ermanno Bencivenga

UNIVERSITY OF CALIFORNIA PRESS

Berkeley • *Los Angeles* • *London*

University of California Press
Berkeley and Los Angeles, California

University of California Press
London, England

Library of Congress Cataloging-in-Publication
Data

Bencivenga, Ermanno, 1950–
    A theory of language and mind / Ermanno Bencivenga.
        p.   cm.
    Includes bibliographical references.
    ISBN 0-520-20791-2 (cloth : alk. paper)
    1. Language and languages—Philosophy.   2. Philosophy of mind.
3. Metaphysics.   I. Title.
B3613.B3835T48   1997
401'.9—dc21   96-48498
                                                                        CIP

Printed in the United States of America

1 2 3 4 5 6 7 8 9

Preface

This book could not have been written if there were not many voices speaking inside of me, voices that belong to "others." Probably the same may be said by any author, but most definitely by this one. And the book would not have been written in the way it was if a number of friends had not cared for it and had not been willing to play with it. It's natural to remember them now and to offer the book to them: more than any other friends or enemies, they should be able to find something of themselves in these pages. And it's a pleasure as well as a duty to thank them: Kent Baldner, Jeff Barrett, Nuccia Bencivenga, Daniel Berthold-Bond, Bill Earle, Calvin Normore, Miguel Vatter. One of them thought the book very much a "private" thing and did not want me to share it with the public. But at least two others bring me the best possible evidence that that would not be a wise choice: they show me that if it's done right, not turned into a circus, publishing is a good way of making new friends—friends you have never met, and perhaps never will.

By the way, this is not a textbook either.

Irvine, June 1996

0   The theory of language and mind presented here is a dialectical one.

0.1   So it will not attempt to define either language or mind by genus and differentia: by listing a number of traits that must belong to whatever is to count as language or mind and that jointly represent (the totality of) what is characteristic (essential?) to language or mind.

0.11 This analytic logic is hopeless: either you get something so general that it does not distinguish between (say) language and lots of other things (think of the "general ideas" of a cat and a dog—of Berkeley's objections to Locke), or you multiply meanings for the word "language," make the word *ambiguous, equivocal.* Just as in dictionaries, which are constructed on this (Aristotelian) basis: you have language$_1$, language$_2$, and so on. And then language (pun intended: the misrepresentation of the semantics of the word "language" reflects—and epitomizes—a broad misunderstanding of the workings *of language*) is considered perverse because it creates so many "unnecessary" complications. (Wouldn't it be easier, and wiser, to use a new word whenever something different is meant? Next thing you know, someone is trying to sanitize the area and bring this unruly behavior under control: a "logically perfect language" is afoot.)

0.12 Ambiguity is telling you something important, if only you took it seriously. If you did not quickly dispatch it as a pathology.

0.13 Or if you made the pathology the center of your concerns. The discourse about what it is to suffer, that is—as opposed to the discourse about what it is to function "properly," "naturally." Eventually to discover, maybe, that there is nothing improper or unnatural about suffering. Or indeed that there is—that while revolting cruelty is well within Nature, that doesn't make it less unwelcome there. Not everyone is welcome home; some homes are divided and dysfunctional, they work improperly and hurt people, and they make them evil and eventually drive them away (which does not mean they are not missed and there is no—morbid? here goes sickness again, elevated to a system—longing for a return to them, for *not* feeling welcome, for being hurt).

0.131   "Natural" language is one of these unnatural homes. Lots of strange, vicious relatives there. Exciting ones, too, like those uncles you so badly needed as a boy, in order to become yourself (*that is,* different from yourself).

0.132   There is a strong ideological basis for the automatic association between pathology and deviance. Think for a second, before you blindly buy into it. (Before you curse at the hammer that just hit your thumb; before you invoke quick obliteration on it.)

0.2   The logic here will be Hegelian: the meanings of "language" and "mind" will consist of narratives, indeed of a single, connected narrative (there is, after all, only one concept, though in any specific case we only deal with some portion of it), which *in its unfolding* will proceed to capture all that is ordinarily regarded as falling under "language" and "mind." The narrative will not do its job if something important is left out: along the way, we will have to account for reference and communication, logic and rhetoric, privacy and consciousness, thought and imagination.

0.21   Some of these elements will *contradict* each other; hence in an analytic framework they would end up canceling each other out, or being passed by in favor of their opposites, or, again, splintering the word (and concept) into equivocal doubles. Within our framework, any such contradiction will signal instead a twist in the plot, the necessity of *Aufhebung*—of a new stage that incorporates the previous ones (if only perhaps in a mode of denial: to say that there will have to be room for everything is not to say that it is possible to make everyone happy—sometimes, room can only be found in a torture chamber, among electrodes and pliers).

0.22   What must be accounted for includes the switching from "I" to "it" to "you" to "one" to (especially!) "we" in the telling of the story. Talk of royal or editorial "we" is only a label for an embarrassing explanatory failure. What *we* say here is the result of a constant, difficult negotiation—indeed, struggle—

among all of *us,* and the story will have to uncover the details of this process.

0.221   "America is making enormous sacrifices to maintain its role as the greatest world power well into the next millennium." That is, *some* are making enormous sacrifices (better yet: are being sacrificed) so that *others* can maintain (and even increase) their power. How much fine structure it is possible to hide beneath a collective reference! And how much shame it is possible to elude that way!

0.23   Some other time "we" might tell a different story, and in a way we know it—it is in the back of our mind. But we must also do our best to keep it back there (for all intents and purposes, to forget it), or we would be cheating. For the game to be played right, we must sweat blood to tell the ultimate story: the one after which no more stories will be needed (about the same material).

0.3   As every Hegelian narrative, the present one, too, can only rationalize the existing data: it can make no prediction about future developments. (When that was tried, it failed miserably—causing considerable joy to the wrong people. A mistake we could have done without.) No prediction, at least, that does not amount to reiterating—*repeating*—the narrative, and its point of view, *and* the (mysterious) choice of that point of view (the mysterious "synthetic act" it expresses); hence to turning the future into the (reconstructed, rationalized, normalized) past. In effect, then, the narrative ends where its author is sitting, with what is available (visible) to him.

0.31   A good example of retrodictive Hegelian narratives: the careful analyses conducted at the end of a game of basketball or soccer, to show how rational and necessary it was for the winner to win. If you were actually watching the game, you often got the feeling that it could have gone either way up until the very end—that it all came down to a few fortuitous episodes. And if it had gone a different way, a different tale of necessity would have been told.

0.311   Indeed, this is not just retrodiction. It is more like the (pro-

jected) retrodiction *of a prediction:* I'm going to tell you now
why you had to know, and in some sense did know, that this
was the way it would turn out. (Which resonates with specific
elements of the particular Hegelian story told here: for something to be incorporated in the notion of *who I am,* it will
have to be construed as having been known all along. And
this, of course, is more than a coincidence: it points to the
substantial identity between Hegelian logic and Hegelian phe-
nomenology.)

0.32   So there is no question that the narrative (and its author) will
be superseded, but that task belongs to others. To try to incorporate it, too, into the narrative would be a sordid attempt
at making history, really, end with oneself. Fortunately, no
such attempt ever works.

0.321   Give those Cronoses some big rock to swallow. Bundled up in
a shroud. They won't notice. Others will, when such greedy,
jealous parents have died of indigestion.

0.322   On the other hand, this is not to say that just because others
will have more data available (or even I will, later), necessarily
they (or I) will tell new stories. Many are delighted to forever
"live" in the past, spinning out a decrepit tale.

0.4   There is a beginning to this narrative, an origin to language
and mind. And that, of course, matters. It establishes order
and priorities. It gives one something definite to regret. But
the origin is no more essential to language and mind than any
of the subsequent developments. However much one might
despise them (and "I" do—that is, part of me does), they are
as much language and mind as the origin is.

0.41   This is in no way a reductionist effort; it is rather a genealogi-
cal one. (Nietzsche is the ironical Hegel, less pompous, less
assured of his position in the story, less capable to tell it in
earnest, without shrill sounds. *This* text is more Nietzsche
than Hegel, but Nietzsche is more Hegel than you would like
to believe, than *Nietzsche* would have liked to believe.) And
there is no reason to think of ancestors (in the genealogy) as
in any way "better" than their descendants. Though, of course,

there may be reasons to think that some are—"circular" reasons, reasons that express commitments, as all reasons do.

0.411   Commitments are unfalsifiable, some feisty mules have discovered—and then they made a redoubtable career out of pointing that out with a reproaching finger.

0.4111   It seems that no one can get attention by bringing out some distinctive *features* something has: he must also call those features names, claim that they are *mistakes* of sorts. Doesn't that tell you something about the genesis of ideas, the humus they grow on? Doesn't it tell you that they are born out of anger, that their "discourse" comes mixed with choleric spit? It does *not,* you say? That has nothing to do with what the ideas *are,* but rather with how they are *presented,* you say? Nice try, partner. Read on.

0.5   According to what the narrative says of language, mind, *and* narratives, the self-description provided above is delusive: the point of a narrative, more or less well concealed under its pretense of comprehension, is one of forcing the existing structure (*not* reflecting it—or maybe reflecting it in a distorted mirror as one major way of forcing it) in previously unanticipated directions (which, *because* they are previously unanticipated, may *need* to be anticipated). But if we based on this conclusion an "ingenious" practice of second-guessing ourselves, the result would be (at best) worthless self-promotion. Once again, we must play the game right—limitations, delusions, and all. Or the point it (supposedly) has would be lost.

0.51   "Worthless" is a value judgment, uttered from a specific stage (in the narrative), a specific pulpit. Laughed at by the accountants, those who care about "net *worth*," who think of self-promotion in terms of "there is no such thing as bad press." They also have a stage here, from which they can go on laughing until some other hyenas are ready to sublate their cadavers.

1   There are patterns to human moves.

1.1   Moves are events. They happen, they take time, they begin and end.

1.11   Events are types, not tokens. That is, they can *reoccur: the same* event can happen repeatedly.

1.111   No account is given here of what it is to be (a repetition of) the same event. We are concerned with a logical structure, not with the concrete modalities of its application, we might say with a supercilious sneer (trying to hide the embarrassment we feel, and if we show enough confidence, or are good enough at exploiting the other guy's lack of confidence, we will get away with it).

1.1111   *Does* this structure have application? Shouldn't we say instead that there *isn't any* (literal) repetition? That any alleged repetition is in fact violation, drift, squinting? Well, we want to say that, *too.* What happens is always the outcome of a conflict, always a compromise formation—which is why it is most often (maybe even always) so *different.* But up to a point different tokens are able to sell themselves (to be sold?) as of the same type. *Both* things matter a lot here.

1.112   Repetition is to an event what duration would be to a thing. And you might think of capturing things within an event ontology by associating them with their repeated occurrence (they last as long as the event of their existence is repeated). But you don't want a facile translation to make you miss the crucial difference of emphasis. A thing's stability is an *inertial* property: if no active force is brought to bear on it, the thing will last indefinitely. Repetition, on the other hand, demands an explanation: we frown when the same happening occurs all over again. (Unless, of course, we got used to it, in which case we no longer notice it—no longer notice the work it takes, largely because of how effective that work has been, how good at putting us to sleep.) So if stability is a special case of repetition, it will require an explanation—indeed, a more complicated explanation than a repetition that presents itself as such.

1.2   A sequence of events is a pattern.

1.21   A pattern is a type, too, not a token. (It, too, can reoccur. And we are about to see that there is a lot of metaphysical content to that "can"—as well as to previous ones.)

1.22 No account is given here of what it is to be the same pattern. But (occurrences of) the same pattern need not be constituted by the same events. (Again, repetition is hardly ever literal—and soon it will be clear that it's always "the same" repetition that we are talking about.)

1.3 Each pattern has a certain degree of *strength*, a certain capacity "to hold itself together." You might even say (we do want to say, you may take us as saying) that the pattern *is* "its" degree of strength: for such a definition to work, we must conceive of a sequence as something that is not just given, that must be constantly maintained or it will disintegrate—and no longer be *one* sequence. Think of Descartes's continuous creation, of Kant's second antinomy (all-important steps in the overcoming of the inertial model). Of how tiresome it is to stay alive, morning after uncalled-for morning—and how, consequently, there will come a time when that pattern is broken off. There had better: what an unbearable pain would immortality be! (But, of course, we don't *reason* that way; we believe there must be a *reason* why someone dies—some extraordinary circumstance must be invoked. Again, our whole sense of what does or does not require an explanation is at stake here.)

1.31 And remember: it's not over when it's over, since a pattern is a type. Think of it as forever tending to grab and arrange events—even when it's not (apparently) succeeding *in the least*.

1.311 The strength associated with a pattern may be a vanishing quantity, virtually ineffective, and make the pattern a "purely theoretical," and far-fetched, possibility. One that will perhaps manifest itself in a dream, and startle us, and be judged absurd, and still be frightening in spite (or because) of its absurdity. With an intensity, a vigor, we will not be able "officially" to justify.

1.32 This notion of strength is a primitive one for us, and it introduces a narrative element at the very core of our metaphysics. For telling is connecting, *articulating*, and conversely what is articulated can be told (not necessarily "by us"), and we are saying that a fundamental and irreducible metaphysical factor emerges in an articulation process. (Though concerning how specifically this process [of constituting patterns] works, *we* here have nothing to say.)

1.33   Another way to put it: "Being is will to power." *That is:* "Being is the concept." (And here you see the previous "methodological" remarks reappear as the flesh and blood of our "claims." An analytic logic goes hand in hand with an atomistic ontology—a theory of impassive, resilient, obstinate *objects*. Whereas a dialectical logic resonates [one octave higher!] with a "vitalistic" universe, a universe that *is* life and not—not to begin with, and maybe never—*someone's* life.)

1.331   When being/will to power is understood as we understand it, this being *must* return eternally. Its mode of being must be a relentless (re)assertion of its structure, however (un)successful the (re)assertion might be. That walk in the woods, that time I laughed in the teacher's face, that watching of *Torn Curtain* right after the set theory exam will forever be working to make room for themselves, in exactly the same way they did *once* (some of it is called "memory").

1.3311 (Originally, memory is but an echo, a ripple effect, ranging all the way from perfectly distinct to faint to imperceptible—from "conscious" to "unconscious," we might say, except that this terminology is mystifying, deceptively flat, maliciously inclined to hide complicated confrontations.)

1.4   Whenever it occurs, an event falls into indefinitely many patterns, of varying strength.

1.41   No such pattern is, in any absolute sense (in any sense that is independent of the pattern itself), more legitimate or truer than any other. In particular, an agent is in no (privileged) position to determine the greater legitimacy or truth of a pattern including any of his moves. What goes through the agent's mind (what he "believes"), or what he declares he "wants" to do (and consequently is ready to "take responsibility for"), is certainly not irrelevant or uninteresting but is not definitive either; it is, quite simply, part of the data, part of what must be assigned to a pattern. (There may be ways for the agent's behavior, *inclusive of what he thinks or says about it,* to "stick together" much more strongly than in any story *he* is prepared to give.)

1.411   For example, I don't know that the act I am currently performing "truly" belongs to a pattern of my working out my "philosophical position" rather than to one of settling some "personal accounts." (I don't even know that it makes sense to say that it *only* truly belongs to one such pattern. And indeed it probably doesn't.) Nor, for that matter, does anyone else know—if knowledge is read as indefeasible, as a necessity operator. (But it's much less common to attribute that kind of indefeasibility to the "knowledge" others have of what one is or does. To one's shrink's, maybe? That indeed is what is so devastating about Freud's attitude. Though we will see that it is devastating "in principle only": the outside, public point of view it judges from was there already, in consciousness. Consciousness *is* the publicity—hence the denial—of the self.)

1.4111 Any mention of "history" is disingenuous if it presumes to close issues or controversies by referring to "the" way something came to be—in this case, say, to determine the "true meaning" of one of my moves by referring to "the" history of my behavior, or of human behavior in general. Not if this mention is understood as naming a problem: as bringing out the inevitably historical character of our understanding, the way in which our logic is (a) history.

1.41111 People who don't know the first thing about the specific structure and problems of history often try the former tack—one of many cases of importing foreign terminology as a terroristic device. But (shamefully!) it is in this shady area between poorly understood *distinct* "specialties" (an area where lowlifes prosper, and spies) that culture is most likely to happen: nothing "professional" about it, or reassuring. When it does get reassuring, it's dead. So I end up admiring people I don't respect—and get to blame everyone, for opposite reasons. How convenient!

1.41112 This point is self-applicable. What is given here is one history of language and mind (one *logic* of them)—the one "I" have chosen, or the one that chose me. There is no way of refuting it by citing "empirical data," since any such data always already require a reading (and hence a logic determining that reading). But, of course, there are ways of competing with it, by making alternative proposals—by telling alternative (hi)stories. When that happens, there will be no neutral standpoint from which the issue can be adjudicated, though there will be definite features of each alternative (each will have, say, a certain amount of detail and coherence) that will sometimes (for some) make a difference. For the idealists among (in) us, *when* their idealism is acting up. That is, when it's not stifled by the partisan projection of one view into something external to all views—something no view can call in question. (That there be an external recourse that establishes the truth of a story *is* transcendental realism—and never mind if we cannot use that recourse to reach actual determinations of truth [or falsity]. It's not *these* practical matters that are at stake here. It's one thing to decide, say, how to describe the sort of person we would want to be a member of the Supreme Court, and quite another to decide how to find out that a given person [best] fits that description. Both, of course, are important political issues.)

1.412   The manifold has priority here. We reject the view that the many presuppose the one; specifically, that the manifold of "my" actions presupposes the unity of my person. Unity follows (when indeed it does) from multiplicity, and it requires considerable effort to keep it in place. (A lot more work must be done for that "my" to make sense. Self-identity cannot be bought at a discount store, or it will show its cheapness. It will rust easily, and crack. And you will wonder about that outcome—talk emptily about "metal fatigue." Trying to dispel the uncanny feeling that has taken possession of you, all of a sudden.)

1.4121   So the sense of familiarity encouraged by some of our initial statements (there are individual events, and they form patterns) is immediately challenged. We already know of a sense in which a "single" event is a manifold: it is a type. Now we have also seen that "the same" event belongs simultaneously to different patterns. Depending on which one it belongs to, can we expect it to always remain "the same"? Or isn't it rather that different patterns will determine different identity conditions for it, hence also determine differently what its *repetition* amounts to? Isn't "the same" event, then, simultaneously *many* events? And doesn't each of those many events resemble a *pattern*, a way for the event to be "shaped," to be "modeled"? It is along such lines that we arrive at the following position: Events are already patterns. The two differ as roles, not as distinct kinds of entities.

1.4122 "Zebras are striped because they are social animals. In the presence of a predator they close ranks, and the predator cannot tell where one animal ends and another begins." *Does* one animal end and another begin? Is the predator *wrong* then? How is that to be understood?

1.413   The view we reject is by far the most popular. In a world dominated by this view, a world made of ones, the manifold is proscribed. Multiplicity is given a bad name and often ends up living down to it, deserving it. (The schizophrenic is not really human—is not rational, is a brute—*therefore* he must be put behind bars. Which eventually *makes* him a brute: a nice case where philosophy does not just understand the world, but changes it, too—for the worse.)

1.4131 So multiplicity rears its (ugly? ugly for whom?) head in all sorts of paradoxical situations, for example, the heap. Confounding the sillies who struggle to define a "logic of vague predicates" and can get nowhere with it. And are surprised to find out that vagueness is itself (second-order) vague, that there is no escaping from it. (Once again, language is telling you something, and what you do is silence it, streamline it. Or, better, try to—since it's not going to work.)

1.41311 But this confusion serves a purpose. It is a tactic. Who knows how much of a mess the sillies could make if they turned their (often considerable) brains away from silly, desperate brain twisters? Unsolvables are intrinsically reactionary. (Though less so than lethargy: strange things might come to mind while trying to "resolve" the liar—and before dying of it. Prisons may nurture the most violent and effective seeds of rebellion. "More" "about" "this" "later.")

1.414   This politics justifies our tone. Some of our tone, at least:

there are (small, vociferous) contexts (like those petulant little dogs, with makeup and ribbons—and cute little pants too!) in which "postmodernism" and multiplicity (allegedly) rule, so there will have to be places below where a different tune is sung. It doesn't take long for onetime revolutionaries to become tyrants (as they continue to use the words that got them there in the first place—and have now been taken for a ride); so we must be on our toes. You never win the battle for freedom, though you can certainly lose it, especially when it looks (to you? remember: there are a lot of frauds out there, a lot of wanting certain things to fail—that is, acting that way—while unctuously displaying the best "intentions") like you won.

1.415   But isn't the dilemma between unity and multiplicity a false one? Shouldn't the two "dialectically" implicate each other? Yes, and thus yield a *unity* of unity and multiplicity! (What a pathetic, laughable stratagem!) Beware of unity trying to win the game after all: assigning the many the subordinate role of a slice in the *one* cake—possibly at the metalevel. Ours is indeed a dialectic, not a dialectical unity but a dialectical *tension:* between the many and the forces that bring them together—those forces that aim at unity but can never, *finally,* "realize" it, indeed, can only make multiplicity more apparent. Subscribing to a higher level of "integration" would be selling out. (The man Hegel might not have liked this. But he doesn't have the last word here, or the first one either—only a few important ones in between.)

1.4151   And isn't the priority of multiplicity just as problematic as that of unity? Shouldn't we abandon the very logic of this confrontation? Beware of unity wanting to cancel the game when its success becomes uncertain—better, wanting to stall it indefinitely, and wait in the wings for its opponent to come back into the (murderous) fold. But we (in the plural!) are not going to fall for that; we too want our day in the sun.

1.4152   You have a hard time seeing things this way? Think of the antithesis of the second antinomy once again: of the world being divisible all the way down. Think of *that* as being how it starts—and stays, underneath (and despite) all presumptuous declarations of victory and all dull acquiescence in them.

1.41521 Kant calls this dull acquiescence (this passivity: the extent to which one *is not*, is no will to power) the "faculty" of sensibility. And he says that sensibility faces the infinitely divisible manifold and that reason/understanding attempts to unify it. All of this must be carefully unpacked, or it will end up sending the wrong messages. We are passive (that is, exercise the faculty of sensibility) to the extent that we offer no resistance to the multiple *external* patterns clamoring for recognition— and can assign no priorities, make no *choices* among them (which is precisely what makes them external, foreign to us). We are active with respect to that multiplicity (that is, exercise the faculty of understanding) to the extent that we identify with a specific (internal) pattern (a pattern that is *what we are*), and fight for its integrity against all other patterns— thus bringing difference into sharp relief. Any apparent success in this fight may be delusive: the pattern we (successfully) fight for may be incorporated in a larger (external) one—one we have not chosen. The faculty of reason requires us to be *absolutely* active, that is, to identify with a universal pattern (one that cannot be so incorporated). Since this kind of identification is impossible, what aiming at it leaves us with is the adoption of a constant critical (and destructive) stance with respect to any specific pattern we have in fact identified with. Therefore the rhetoric of establishing unity goes together with a practice of radicalizing division, and conversely a purely passive acceptance of division has the effect (not certainly of eliminating it altogether, but at least) of minimizing its impact—reducing the urgency of the struggle, moving it as far as possible toward sheer side-by-sideness. (In this sense, we agree that the real is rational: the activity of reason—activity *as* reason—brings out the multiplicity that being is, it makes being come forward as the multiplicity it is, it manifests its "nature." That activity and this nature resonate with each other. When, however, the same slogan is understood more conventionally, making reason side with *achieved, actual* unity, we can only see it as a reactionary tool.)

1.42   There is competition between any two patterns encompassing
          the same event. (Yes, even between a pattern and any of its
          components: each of the latter is calling attention to itself and
          threatening to explode the "parent" pattern. There is no en-
          compassing that is not also an imprisoning, and no "falling
          under" that is not also attempting to undermine. With
          friends—or disciples, or teachers—like this, . . .) In the com-
          petition, the strength of each pattern is expended.

1.421   Economic jargon and strategies become relevant now: since
          strength can be *expended,* it can also be *managed, saved,*
          capitalized, distributed, and, of course, *wasted.*

1.422   And so do, clearly, political jargon and strategies: since
          strength can be expended, it can also *force* certain outcomes,
          and *oppose* certain others, and itself *be opposed* by equal or
          unequal strength. Various hierarchical, associative, or antago-
          nistic relations may emerge as a result. Various "forms of gov-
          ernment," as one might call them (since it is, after all, an issue
          of administering power), with various goals—and various de-
          grees of success and stability, depending on how well their
          "economy" is managed.

1.5   The same events and patterns can occur anywhere, in any me-
          dium.

1.51   Therefore no move or pattern belongs to a specific agent.
          Whatever its origin, it can always be (mis?)appropriated by
          anyone and turned to "unintended," even inimical purposes.
          (There will be those who say that Mozart "ought not" to be
          used to sell insurance or low-sodium crackers. They will say
          it with an anxious tone, in the name of the "integrity" of the
          work of art—or, seriously now, of *their own* integrity, which
          they feel to be threatened by this bad example of seepage. Bad
          because it is an example, and an example because it is seep-
          age: exemplarity *is* seepage.)

1.511   (There are also those who are always afraid of being quoted
          "out of context." They have little confidence that their pat-
          terns will be able to defend themselves outside the little shells
          where they have found a comfortable home.)

2   Patterns may become entrenched.

2.1   Some patterns are in fact repeated (the same pattern, which, we know, *can* occur again, does). Events (moves) are not thereby "locked" into a single (repeated) pattern: multiplicity is still there, though repetition might make it less conspicuous. (Also, there may be several repeated patterns including the same events, some more conspicuous than others, as a consequence of their different strength and economic proficiency. Some may be forced underground, and, when they come up for air, bewildered denial will often be a last-ditch defense: "How come I always find myself doing the same idiotic thing?" Or, more elaborately, "What's wrong with me? Why do I persist in acting so self-destructively?"—that is, why is "my" acting so destructive of the simpleminded idea of a "self" that most often gets "me" through the night? Finally, remember: there might be no literal repetition, it might be that what is called repetition always has an element of novelty, of transgression, that calling it repetition is itself an ideological move. But that very ideology and the fact that it sticks are indications that the *drive* to repetition is there, and that, though possibly never completely successful, this drive is often successful enough—enough to force a certain description of the situation, if nothing else.)

2.11 "Conspicuous" as a new primitive term? Not at all: it can be defined in terms of the competition among patterns, and of its outcomes. A pattern is conspicuous insofar as it is a winner in that competition. (So a repeated pattern is one that has enough comparative strength to emerge as a winner over and over again.)

2.111 That the competition revolve about—and its prize consist in—*visibility* is an important commentary on this allegedly least offensive (and most "disinterested") of senses. Whose significance will not be lost on the children whose (various) potentials could not flourish because the relevant patterns were not strong enough to impose themselves onto the environment's lack of concern (to *grab* a sizable portion of the environment). The underachievers who ended up looking like wallpaper—entirely swallowed by an extrinsic motif. Sometimes spitefully disgorging their long dammed-up energy (in relatively trivial modes, which, of course, will not help their cause: they will just be regarded as wallpaper of a different kind).

2.12   Conspicuousness must not be understood as the property a pattern has when someone is (or many are) *conscious* of it. I automatically avoid all sorts of obstacles as I walk (they are conspicuous enough to influence my behavior) without experiencing any of the focused attention and the reflexivity that seem to be definitional of consciousness. More generally, I see and hear all sorts of things, and act on the basis of what I see and hear, without being conscious of any of it. Of course, I *could* become conscious of it; but that would belong to a different and more tortuous situation, where different and more tortuous abilities come into play. And, of course, you will say that I was all along "subliminally" conscious of it—"unconsciously conscious," that is—and I will read your awkward statement as an indication that a power play is going on, that an ideologically based *re*construction of my life (and my "experience," too!) is trying to extend its domination on older and refractory ground.

2.2   A repeated pattern must have some reproductive advantage over the competition: its strength and the ways it is administered must favor it in survival terms. But no extravagant conclusions are warranted about the "larger meaning" of this outcome. This is no technology of (providential) creation, no tool in the hands of a benevolent master.

2.21   There are many blind alleys to evolution: many things that are so only because there is no reason why they should be otherwise (or no good reason—think of the wings of the argus pheasant and in general of how sexual selection explodes the whole notion of an increasing adaptiveness: you must, besides "natural" selection, also admit, . . . yes, this *unnatural* kind; and once you admit that, the whole game is over, though it may take you a while to realize it). There are also many branches that get stunted, independently of how adaptive they *might have been* (had the story been told differently, had there been a place from which a different story could be told). In the end, it's all so very stupid: so stupidly self-serving. Quite effective, too, as stupid things (and people) often are. (Effectiveness may just *be* stupidity: "lack of power to absorb ideas or impressions." You may *have to* shut your ears to what else is happening, in order to be effective.) Cruel, too.

2.211   *Tuez-les tous: Dieu reconnaîtra les siens.* A simple, even witty recipe. It cuts down on the amount of red tape; it avoids lengthy explanations, subtle *distinguos.* You have better things to do with your time. (Like looking nice on your golf cart.)

2.22   "Evolution" is the wrong word.

2.23   Worse: using that word is a form of demagogic propaganda. It makes you feel good about existing things. It makes you think of what does not exist as a lower form, one that didn't deserve to exist.

2.24   "Existing" is a value judgment. It validates a selection process that distills a single line in a maze and then imposes it as what "is the case." "Nonadaptive" amounts to "(temporary?) loser in a power struggle." And I mean here: a power struggle (and a selection process) *among narratives,* among (possible) histories. Among patterns.

2.241   There is nothing strange about that: "the world" contains such power struggles (indeed, is made of them, though you often don't see them—though making you not see them is part of how they are fought, and won), hence adapting to the world requires adapting to them. A youth in south central L.A. must adapt not only to a drug- and gang-infested environment but also to a bunch of tales (not necessarily *told* by anyone) about the inevitability of his condition (and to how those tales inevitably contribute to shaping the environment). The ordinary understanding of "adaptive" tends to forget such matters—thus creating more (apparent, but then, because of that, also real) stability. It tends to transform the competition of narratives into a narrative of competition. Written by the survivors, in the name and for the greater glory of survival.

2.3   The more a pattern is repeated, the more likely it is that it will be repeated again.

2.31   If you won once, it will cost you less next time around. And
         it will cost others more to resist you. ("Never underestimate
         the heart of a champion!" In some sense, champions have
         hearts like anyone else, but it doesn't look that way. And
         therefore it isn't.)

2.311   (There is something nontrivial about the old saw "appearance
         is reality": some interesting structure, some genuine insight
         into how it all works. It's not just a self-refuting, "skeptical"
         bit of cleverness.)

2.4   A pattern that is repeated often tends to become more pre-
         dictable.

2.41   That is, it tends to recur whenever certain circumstances
         arise. It tends to "complete" those circumstances in a stan-
         dard way.

2.411   From the moment he opens his mouth, there is no stopping
         his routine. And that's largely because of how many times he
         ran it, without sensible opposition (only a tired smile, some
         yawning—nothing he would be forced to come to terms with,
         to act on).

2.42   And, consequently, it is expected when those circumstances
         arise.

2.421   There are subjective resonances to "expected" and "predict-
         able," to which we are *not* committed. And yet we will con-
         tinue to use this terminology.

2.422   We are working with words laden with abusive ideologies.

2.4221   Why abusive? Because they have carried the day for so long,
         which makes for complacency and arrogance.

2.4222   Clearly, open confrontation is favored here, though in general
         it requires more of an expenditure than an established power
         structure. Could it be that "I" favor a general economy, an
         economy of waste? I'd say, Yes. But there is more going on
         (and being favored) than what "I" favor. Even in me.

2.423   It would be hopeless (and wrong), however, to attempt a re-
         turn to some pure, innocent state. What we need instead is to
         reclaim those words. Expose the abuse and its background;

write a new chapter in this development. Continue the development, move forward into the future, though (our story
about) the past may be our driving force.

2.4231   Make some of the stunted branches grow again? Give them
         (us?) another chance?

2.4232   And encourage *their* eventual complacency and arrogance?
         There is no way of keeping one's hands clean. Which doesn't
         mean you ought not to try. (You most definitely ought to; in
         fact, that's the whole significance of an "ought." Only impos-
         sible tasks—tasks *perceived, experienced* as impossible—
         make you appreciate that significance; only then do you have
         to choose for or against, and can you not play games with
         yourself. Can you not phrase your agenda in the indicative
         mood. Pretend to be "realistic.") You ought to be always
         ready to chastise your former friends—and your former
         selves. To stand firm before their puzzled stare, or their sud-
         den rage. Knowing full well how much you contributed to
         bringing about their undeserved fortune, and how much you
         will do more of the same in the future.

2.424   We don't want to use *new* words either. We can easily see
         through that dividing and conquering strategy. Through the
         delusive "peace" it brings—the peace of death finally im-
         posed on the enemy. (The hypocrisy of "hyphenated Ameri-
         cans"!) Each in his little cubicle, forever disconnected, and
         hence forever harmless. Clawless, weaponless. Though possi-
         bly hooked to the Internet (the only thing that is still con-
         nected, and is enjoying great power as a result—at our ex-
         pense).

2.4241   While we play the game of fragmentation—a game for rich,
         decadent kids (lemmings judiciously engaged in transcenden-
         tal suicide)—systematicity (the ability to master complex pat-
         terns and turn multiplicity to one's evolutionary advantage;
         the carrot that drives reason's mercilessly destructive action)
         is re-created at a different level. Where we don't even see it,
         where we don't expect to see it, where we expect only ma-
         chinic, "soulless" aggregation. Are we in for a surprise! (Of
         course not, you will say: science fiction has been describing
         things like that for ages. And you don't reflect on the impor-

tance of calling it "fiction"—or, on the contrary, of bringing it into a "serious" context. Nor do you reflect on the meaning of your smug dismissal.)

2.4242   What's wrong with *dividing* and conquering? you will ask. Aren't we suppose to side with multiplicity here? And then I will have to repeat (literally?) that what's wrong is the conquering, and that the relation between the two is not accidental: dividing is one of the best ways of *unifying* (things *as* divided). Which, I will also insist, is not necessarily all bad for all the characters in *this* story (but it is for me, insofar as what I am talking about is a specific danger of being conquered).

2.425   In due time, we will know what "subjective" means. And that it matters—and why.

2.5   Past a certain threshold of predictability, a pattern is entrenched. That is: it is possible to use its predictable character, *even in the presence of conspicuous exceptions,* as a strength-saving resource. Or (the other way around): an entrenched pattern is one that is predictable enough for exceptions to it to be acknowledged (it is in this sense that the exception proves the rule: only something acknowledged as a rule can have something acknowledged as an exception).

2.51   "He's not even consistent enough with his shot yet to be inconsistent," says a sportswriter of a basketball player.

2.52   Nothing is said here about the nature or location of the threshold.

2.521   Lots of things are not said here. But that much *is said,* not papered over by some vague reference to what is "intuitive" or "obvious." Which is another way of not saying, without admitting to it—another way of not doing the work that philosophy *is.* Work that will go through you, that will happen anyway, that you will not be able to restrain. Thank God! (God must be a philosopher.)

2.5211   (Else how could He create? And why would He need to rest if creation was not hard, merciless work?)

2.5212   There is, of course, a residue of contingency to any attempt at an explanation, but that is precisely the *limit* of any such attempt. You may call it an insurmountable limit, and even congratulate yourself for having reached it, if it makes you feel better; but it will be surmounted, and you know it. The explanation (the story, the poetry—or the dialectic—of it) will continue to unfold, *backward* and forward. Though it may be stalled indefinitely, as long as those who feel comfortable with its present stage are able to sell their limits as "hard facts." Using whatever promotes their cause, for example, laughing at the arguments of the "philosophy of nature"—trying not to understand, and to make no one understand, what heroic, precious work those arguments are doing.

2.53   An entrenched pattern may lose any reason it originally had for repetition (any "advantageous" feature). Its being entrenched will in general guarantee its repetition anyway. Even if there was *no* reason for it; even if the only "reason" for it was that there was no reason against it. (For us, of course, that is itself a good reason: if the competition lags, patterns will assert themselves.)

2.54   Reality—in one of its incarnations, another name for conspicuousness—has a snowballing effect: that it occupies space and time makes it occupy *more* of them.

2.541   That I have a chance to busy myself with intellectual matters is enough of an "argument" for continuing to have this chance, *and for denying it to others.* I am better at it because *I am* at it. (Where the "because" signals a logical connection, not an empirical one—as in, "Within transcendental idealism, there are objects *because* presentations are coherent, connected, and so on." Nothing is learned by this statement other than how certain words *must* be used. Of course, we don't yet know what "logic" is—but it begins to dawn on us that it has to do with the military, with the enforcement of discipline, with boot camps and shouting orders. Not necessarily because it espouses that life-form: all I am saying is that it must engage it. I am saying that in logic the problem of freedom *is posed.* Within the empirical realm, on the other hand, freedom is no longer an issue: what issue it was has been decided, so we can emptily and happily proceed to "find out" about this and that.)

2.5411   A morality for bigots, and for the faint at heart. Courage was
         a virtue once, remember (indeed, it was virtue itself, *virtus*),
         and it's not because of Vietnam and the like that it's now
         laughed out of court. (The battlefield was only, at best, a
         source of evidence for it—ambivalent, as all evidence is.) The
         matter is much deeper, and slimier. Courage has been carica-
         tured, cartooned to death: it is all over the place (that is, talk
         of it is) so no one will notice its absence. (Not only can ab-
         sence be a mode of presence; the reverse may be true as well.)
         Rambo will provide an alibi for universal cowardice. For the
         universal incapacity to sustain the most trivial choice, even if
         it is a choice in favor of (the flight toward) "reality." Most
         cowards don't even have the courage of their cowardice. (Is
         that what is cowardly about them? I guess there could be a
         courageous way of being cowardly, and hence not cowardly
         after all. I guess that's what makes the terrified characters of
         some war movies "good guys": they have [boldly] *chosen* to
         be terrified. Though, after a while, it no longer works: it, too,
         has become a cliché—since it no longer requires any choice,
         it is now standard practice, *vulgar* standard practice.)

2.5412   Indeed, not a morality at all, *and hence* a morality. Originally,
         morality speaks with (and from) resentment, regret, reproach,
         envy—with (and from) the many voices of nothing. Then it
         is (dialectically) violated, and becomes justificatory in nature.
         Harmonious, contented, self-satisfied. The ca(n)nons are
         turned around and made to fire against "one's own" people—
         who at that point, because of that move, are no longer one's
         own. No longer in the same sense (in the sense of "one's own
         car" as opposed to "one's own conviction," of "owning some-
         thing" as opposed to "owning *up to* it").

2.5413   It takes a long, roundabout, dialectical journey to go from the
         morality of Greek tragedies (where gods themselves resent
         human happiness—look at *The Trojan Women*, for example,
         where Athena turns against the Greeks, for specious reasons,
         as soon as they have finally won the war) to one in which kids
         are educated to be pleased by the "good fortune" of others.
         (We are talking about ideals, of course, not statistical compli-
         ance—let alone spontaneous, unresisting compliance.) Would

there be less depression if envy were not so openly dis*owned?* (There are those who take ideals seriously, you know, and let themselves be tormented by them.)

2.542 Eventually, the workings of the selection that established reality become virtually unretrievable. Things *become* existing, indeed. I *become* an intellectual, in the sense that I become such that I *have always been* an intellectual (and those other losers were *never* good enough). All the other allegiances my moves had (and still have) are now invisible. (More so from afar, though: when you get closer, a number of surprising little obscenities surface. It seems odd that somebody like that should even be associated with intellectual practices. That disgusting old lecher. Therefore, discretion is the best way to work at one's biography—in case you are willing to trade your life for a hardbound book ["Absolutely not—only if I get a paperback edition too!"], or have enough power to manipulate the media and force them to be discreet anyway.) "There is" by now but one pattern, the best possible one. Candide has come to life—*and is no joke.*

2.55 Reality has a solid, tyrannical advantage over the unreal. Better: having that advantage *is* reality. So how do I speak about what preceded—and still suffers from—this tyranny, about that other reality on which the real is based, which the real has made unreal? I just do, and screw the "contradiction." Screw what selfishness calls "impossibilities" (or "necessities"). ("You can't run a red light." "Just watch me.")

2.551 "Life is unfair." Or: the most devastating realistic statement. What can you say to that—if indeed you are a realist? What can you do? Cry?

2.552 Think of how many "revolutions" (were) aborted. And how they are considered wrong because of that.

2.553 The failure of communism, stupid! It took them seventy years to realize it wouldn't work! To "realize" it, indeed. *Could* it work now, given that it *is* no longer? (Or is it rather that now is when it could work best, when we should finally take it seriously—now that its odious travesties have been exploded

and can no longer be used as convenient excuses? Was it perhaps the notion of "real" that caused all the problems, in
"real socialism"?)

2.554   Ideals are wishful thinking, you say. Ideality is immaturity,
        childishness. No need of arguing against it; slander and sar-
        casm will be enough. It is enough to embarrass the idealist, to
        make him stutter. And the damned fool *will* stutter: after all,
        he's an accomplice, any day of the week—any weekday (a
        cute, sneaky little game is played with that word; thumbs are
        fingers, or you wouldn't have ten of the latter, and weeks in-
        clude holidays—[week]ends, goals, are part of *everyday* life).

2.555   Gramsci had it all wrong. Machiavelli loomed too large for
        him. Survival is only survival. A long period of time is only a
        long period of time. Nothing follows from the fact that a pro-
        gram failed—except that it failed. Beware of penalizing it
        twice! And nothing follows from the fact that people buy cer-
        tain things. It certainly doesn't follow that they need them, or
        that those things are useful or valuable. Think of pet rocks
        before you idolize the market. Before you call it "optimal."
        Before you judge everything else according to how well it
        matches its workings.

2.5551 The ultimate example of prostitution: the market of ideas.
        If you want to be buggered, just keep on walking backward.
        You may be sure that someone will accommodate you.

2.5552 If you stick to an idea (a pattern), however unsuccessful you
        might be, the idea will have at least as much conspicuousness
        as your choice gave it. If you betray it, it won't even have that.
        (I know, I know: someone's "betrayal" is someone else's "as-
        tute negotiation, promoting the idea's better future." I can't
        give you a single recipe to decide all individual cases; I can
        only discuss the meaning of certain general attitudes—the
        ways certain general words relate to other general words.
        Every time *I* handle an individual case, the stories I tell myself
        about it must be much more specific and context-dependent,
        hence also much harder to project onto different contexts.
        And then, also, in individual cases I have to act, which means
        stop telling stories, accept the fact that I do not understand,

that understanding—that is, playing—is a luxury I cannot afford.)

3   The violation of an entrenched pattern is painful.

3.1   An entrenched pattern is violated if it does not occur when expected. (Remember: no subjective content to this talk of expectedness.)

3.11   Expectation of an entrenched pattern is not necessarily absolute (the pattern will in general have only a statistically significant degree of recurrence). So violations will also be matters of degree. There may be no (conspicuous) violation if a given recurring pattern does not recur just once, but the more it does not recur, the more this will be a violation.

3.12   All sorts of ploys can help insulate violations (and deprive them of impact). That such ploys are often perfectly trivial does not detract from their effectiveness. (Effectiveness and stupidity, once again: it's amazing how inane the explanations are that people are willing to confidently, indeed enthusiastically, endorse. Or *is* it amazing? Which of course is the whole point.) Thus it often "works" to call something an exception (whatever that means)—as does to call it an anomaly, a nonstandard occurrence, a dream, a hallucination.

3.2   An undesirable state (called "pain": the undesirable *as such*) characterizes any (admitted) violation of an entrenched pattern (you can think of it, to begin with, as an expression of the sudden need for applying strength—but soon this pain will acquire other meanings and roles), whether or not any (additional) undesirable consequences also follow from the violation (that is, whether or not the entrenchment of the pattern has been "damaged" in a more or less permanent way).

3.21   I may or may not be hurt when I violate some of my ordinary routines. (I mishandle a knife and cut myself, and bleed. Or I just come up with a lovely new trick and derive vast profits from it. Or both—and I bleed all the way to the bank.) Whether or not I am hurt, there will be some discomfort to the violation per se.

3.22   Reality knows how to make itself heard, how to protect itself from unreality, how to *keep* unreality unreal. (Here is the main secondary use of the sudden rush of adrenaline, and of the temporary agony that goes with it: it makes it possible to economize while being forced to spend—indeed, to turn the very process of spending to that effect! Remember Freud: anxiety turned into a signal.)

3.221   I have already said something like that, under a different number! Yes, and that's how it should be. This whole numbering system is clearly Aristotelian; so there will have to be a reappearance of the same themes in various locations to bring out its limits. Cross-references as a main weapon for guerrilla warfare.

3.2211   Repetition again, this time with a saving character? It all depends, as usual, on who (or what) is being saved. Each conflicting pattern aims at its own repetition, and all these repetitions are in conflict: every one of them will tend to (at least partially) inhibit the others. In the present case we have a hierarchical (Aristotelian) structure incorporating what it can and rejecting all the rest. *And* we have what is incorporated or rejected putting up a fight—*for example,* by recurring here and there, in ways that the structure cannot easily account for. Depending on which side you are on, you will or will not look at the latter recurrence with sympathy and approval.

3.2212   Thus a book will often contain ferocious enemies within its own bounds. Wonder why certain *very self-consciously* "(self-)deconstructive" books have no index? No bibliography? Hard-to-track-down references? (It's a matter of national tradition, you say? Funny it should extend to translations then. Is it out of respect? Or laziness? Or something worse?)

3.2213   Think of the kind of book you will have to write if you want to make sure that it's *read,* when cross-references are generated electronically in a split second for every text—not just those unfortunate enough to be too famous (those no one has been reading for a *long* time). Think of how you will have to hide your "meaning" under the most unpredictable words, the least obvious ones (which probably means the least specific, the most unqualified—articles and prepositions, maybe?), so that thorough "searches" might turn up empty-handed and people might actually be forced to face your text in the order you intended them to.

3.2214 But why then adopt this numbering system in the first place? (Why favor this kind of repetition?) For more than one reason. (Indeed, too many of them, which makes me wonder who is really speaking here.) We must try different paths to "the same" destination, to get to know the territory better. We must try *this* path, precisely because it is so old and respectable. (We want to be respected, too, and deserve to be, and are not going to offer opponents any cheap way out. We know our Aristotelian logic, and can reveal its defects from the inside.) We understand ourselves better when using a tool that offers resistance, when forced to be sagacious and resourceful. And, finally, no resistance makes for no action: if it were not for the resistance, we might as well not write at all. (Which, often, is exactly what happens, though the resulting "activity" is still called "writing." Providing a nice cover for the most awful obtuseness, and the most pervasive totalitarianism.)

3.22141 (I have seen writing taught by people who never wrote anything themselves, but had all sorts of ingenious strategies to recommend to others. To make sure that they too would never write. *Whatever* they did—and especially if what they did was called "writing.")

3.23 There is something intrinsically reassuring and comforting about the status quo. Even a status quo we firmly believe could—or should—be better. Even one that horrifies us.

3.231 "We must be doing something right, to last two hundred years." Yes, and (y)our Parthenon is better preserved than the one in Athens—and so much closer. And all those pretty Austrian villages next to Mauthausen, with the railroad tracks going right through them.

3.2311 Is this telling me something about beauty? I think it is; I know I will have to go back to it (it will recur again; there is no way of getting rid of it).

3.232   "Don't make waves." You might drown. (On the other hand, you might drown anyway.)

3.233   "When do we start having fun?"

3.24   Anxiety accompanies any news.

3.241   Not surprisingly, if anxiety is the announcement of fragmentation. Pain without pain; pain with nothing to show for it (a nice deep wound, an amputated limb, a rotten tooth, a newborn); the pain that best reveals the *nature* of pain. The sign of the (re)emergence of multiplicity: of this little game about to be knocked down, suddenly in need of support.

3.242   So "the news" will have to feel old, if advertising money is to be made.

3.2421   There is nothing more predictable (objectively *and* subjectively—whatever that means, whatever *you* mean by that) than the news format. Two minutes of this, five minutes of that. It is as good an example as any of an entrenched pattern. You go to sleep in front of massacres and famine. And have pleasant dreams, whether your eyes are closed or open.

3.2422   And you turn ugly when they try to wake you up. "They don't have the right to bother me! To intrude into my space!" (Or, "I'm doing nothing wrong. I'm just having a good time.")

3.24221   (Analogously: "I just happen to like expensive meals and clothes, and I am paying for them with my own money. What's the problem with that? Whom am I hurting? I am still a leftist." This is definitely not a digression.)

3.2423   "The news" is a reassuring expression. Doubly reassuring, indeed—and deceptive. It reassures you while it seems to unsettle you and thus deflates unsettling itself. (As universities do, and museums: they let you think that you are making room for "culture" and "art," that you are wise and brave and tolerant. And guess what: brutal censorship and repression usually do a better job—not for you, of course, not for those who think as you do. The most effective way to handle your troubled and troublesome self may be to destroy you. The Mafia understood that very well: a bullet zigzagging through a brain goes a lot farther than any complicated negotiations with[in] the brain's owner. But not always can one afford this straight-forward resolution. So it's best to have a wide, diversified array of weapons available, which is confusing, *and the confusion is an additional weapon.*)

3.24231   ("What we are doing must be somehow terribly relevant and radical, if they are so eager to cut our funds." Yeah, you are supposed to think that—that's one way they neutralize what you *could* be doing. *In addition* to threatening cuts *and* to encouraging your increasing irrelevance. All are means to the same end.)

3.2424   This is fine, shrewd political action. Because it "goes without saying," and in the process leaves you without a say.

3.2425   Though it doesn't work all the time. If it did, incidentally, there would be no significance to talk of "time." There is time because there is aging, and there is aging because there is a war constantly fought within every one of us (and within everything else).

3.24251   This is Hegel's limit (and Nietzsche's main contribution): he had no explanation for why the dialectical process would have to take time—why it couldn't occur all at once, in a flash. He talked about this process as involving hard work, of course, but did not account for the necessity of that work. Because he did not see that there are *several* dialectical processes going on, each offering resistance to all the others, refusing to be encompassed by them and trying to be the one that does the encompassing. Each constituting (part of) the *prime matter,* (of) the *medium,* where the others must assert themselves. (That is what is opaque about matter, what *makes* it matter: not that it has no structure but that we cannot recognize its structure, which is some *other* structure, some structure we have not been able to assimilate. We cannot make it so much of a concession, allow it so much dignity, or we would already be halfway toward losing to it.)

3.243   But are novelty and change always painful? Some people perceive them (within certain limits) as pleasurable. Answer: only painful things can be pleasurable. There is no radical opposition between pleasure and pain (indeed, the two are often difficult to tell apart), but there is between indifference and pain (which can give rise to pleasure, by being overcome—in the sense of *aufgehoben*: canceled *and* preserved). So when it comes to demanding activities also regarded as engaging and gratifying (mathematics, chess, reading something that is not pulp fiction—that is not entirely "by the book"), their actual microphysics is that you experience discomfort here and there, and find yourself able to handle it (to extend and confirm your patterns), *and that's what the pleasure is all about.*

3.2431   Eventually, we might learn to do this in a systematic way. We might discover the advantages of disciplined effort in handling internal sources of discomfort—primarily boredom, which follows upon the lack of expected (confirmation and) pleasure: nothing like overstimulating your children if you want them to be perpetually dissatisfied, if you want a general pattern of hyperactivity to grab them and control their lives.

3.24311 Does that amount to *spoiling* them? Or is spoiling them, on the contrary, letting them vegetate in front of the TV set? Notice how much dialectical confrontation surprisingly permeates every word, how there always turn out to be adverse interests at work, trying to appropriate the word. There are even those who think that "overstimulation" applies to what the TV does. They focus on the intensity of the stimuli, at the expense of their variety.

3.3   Unreality exercises constant pressure.

3.31   Unreality is always there. And so, consequently, is pain. You need to be constantly anesthetized against it. Constantly forgetful. Endorphins are an indispensable component of the life process.

3.311   There where? *In* reality. Contra the conventional wisdom, reality (the reality of it) is highly precarious and always on the verge of collapse (think of a fault, of an earthquake in the midst of the quietest night, of little whirls growing into a tornado; and think of all the earthquakes and tornadoes that did *not* happen—that are *waiting to* happen). Any report on reality is a gross oversimplification of a complicated superposition. Which of course has surfaced in our most basic scientific theory (the one fools implicitly refer to when they talk about the great success of "science" and try to build their pet ideology on that "solid foundation")—except that we don't yet know how to reason that way. "Quantum logic" was only a short-lived, superficial evasion (but an important symptom).

3.32   This is not a peaceful and serene garden. We were chased from one such garden long ago, and that act instituted us, our time, and our world. Therefore, we will also never reach that ideal state—not as long as this continues to be our world (and we continue to be *we?*). Though it might help to think of such an ideal, and of what it would mean to reach it, and that we are in some sense "approaching" it.

3.321   Help whom? Both parties, in fact: if the dynamics of your condition can be described as an improvement, you will feel better about what you have, the way you *are*. On the other hand, an improvement is still a change, it is still nonbeing having an impact, showing its power—and it may be that no changes are possible unless they are described that way.

3.322   The same moves may be serving (be owned by) opposite masters. Prolonging their lives and their struggle. Making the struggle possible by helping keep both parties around while also making it real: constituting its very substance, the daily workings of it. (A struggle about *whose* moves these are.)

3.33   Chaos has not been finally vanquished. Cosmos has not been finally established. Violations will happen, "for no reason," however solid and powerful the forces of conservatism might be. Pain and anxiety will invade us.

3.331   In this sense (we know already), all that is real is *not* rational. As you establish the most forcefully when you try to prove otherwise. (But you might be smarter and never do that, and call it quits before you even play—thus purchasing a cheap, shallow, "pragmatist," no-questions-asked form of "rationality." Avoiding the tiresome, relentless "labor of the negative." At the cost of overwhelming, *revealing* boredom, for those of us who *were* overstimulated children. Pragmatism is the negation of philosophy made into a philosophical stance. With an ironically dialectical twist—but the joke is on them!)

3.3311   (Pragmatists are the most consistent and stable absolutists: they are absolutely committed to absolutely nothing, and can maintain that kind of commitment in the face of absolutely everything.)

3.34   It might hit you when you least expect it. So you better learn to expect it.

3.341   From a booklet on how to deal with drunk drivers: expect the unexpected.

3.342   Reality is somewhat intoxicated (to begin with—before it becomes reality, before it becomes what it *is*): as fuzzy as a drunkard's vision, made of several (superposed) patterns.

3.343   Drunkenness is dangerous. It might make you lose "control" (of multiplicity), lose your *one*self. Make you see the ridge you are riding on. Make the ridge speak (and the abyss on both sides). Make you feel the attraction of the abyss (of all that was supposed to be muzzled). You must stay away from this revelation. For "your own" sake, for your own survival, for the sake of survival—which surreptitiously has become "you."

3.3431   And this you might accomplish by doing more of the same. By drinking yourself into a stupor. Too much of anything will kill you—even too much lucidity. (In moderate amounts, an animal's urine is a fertilizer, but too much of it will burn the grass.) And will reestablish a neat division between real and unreal. Making the latter dead, out of commission. No longer a threat. (What's threatening is the *reality* of the unreal—or, for that matter, the unreality of the real. When those are forgotten, when the division is perceived to be a hard-and-fast one, the danger is past. We can breathe again.)

3.34311   Don't try to reduce the whole issue to the injecting or smoking of some chemical substances (and thus to resolve it). Things don't stay put: they go around, making up strange figures, and turn against themselves. (Because they are not, "really," *things*: not the way "realism" conceives of them. "There are no such things.") If you think that drug use per se is an eye-opener, you are (trying to be) foolish. You will never gain that kind of certainty, and you (should) know it.

3.34312   There are no progressive or repressive drugs. There are only drugs that are both.

3.34313   Maybe everything must be both (of something), or it would not be. Maybe everything needs at least two (antagonistic) props to stand up.

3.3432   Advice to tightrope walkers: think that you are always walking in ordinary surroundings, that you are on solid ground. Think that there is nothing you can fall into. Nothing does not exist.

3.34321   Except that it does. *Calling* it nothing is a useful first step toward silencing it.

3.34322   Think of how much power must be enforced before you can even pose the problem of the possibility of a creation "from nothing." Think of what must have been done to nothing before that problem can arise. "Being and nothingness" is an ideological pairing—though it may be the best we can do.

3.34323   "America was virgin land before the arrival of the white man." Or, more viciously (because more cleverly—there is something hateful about this kind of Wall Street, Madison Avenue cleverness, whatever its intent and outcome, and about feeling good about it: it's our rationality rebelling, feeling violated, our rebelliousness feeling dislocated from its rational basis, deprived of it, "rationalized"), "Those other guys were not using the land."

3.35   Better still: you *do* something about it.

4   It pays to perform efficient anticipations of violations. (Pays whom? Everyone, as usual—or it wouldn't be enough. Unilateral payoffs don't provide lasting advantages. Too great a triumph will suffocate you.)

4.1   Given a set S of events, a set T of events is an *abstraction* of S (modulo f) if there is a function f mapping S into T.

4.11   Remember: events don't necessarily "happen," that is, are not necessarily acknowledged, do not necessarily make it to official "reality." Some of the most important ones never do (their great strength is effectively counteracted), and force our language to awkward, absurd convolutions ("parapraxes," "unconscious wishes").

4.111   And when language does (is done) that, it is making its most fruitful contribution. Then something is really going on in (with) language; everything else is dead calm—the dream of a "logic of identity." Which, for some, is capable of (a temporary) realization: they are able to keep things still (for a while)—the things that seem to work for them.

4.112   We haven't introduced language yet, within our narrative; so what we say about it is bound to have a provisional character. "The same" statements acquire different resonances at different stages of the narrative, especially as the narrative proceeds to incorporate them.

4.12   From now on, we will disregard the function *f*. But before we do that, we need to bring out its significance—the crucial element of variability introduced by this parameter.

4.121   In a purely mathematical sense, there is always a function *f* between any two sets (indeed, except in trivial cases, more than one). So, in that sense, any set is an abstraction of any other. If the notion of abstraction is not to be emptied of all content (which would also have a negative effect on every other notion defined in its terms—including anticipation and language), it must not be read mathematically. Nor can it be read phenomenologically, as something that "shows up" in consciousness, because consciousness has no primordial status for us; on the contrary, it is one of the later (and more devious) epicycles of our development. So what we are left with looks like an arbitrary positing: some functions (in the mathematical sense) simply are (posited), and some are not. Of course, *once* they are (posited), they can (and often will) be identified with the (possibly conscious) point of view of a human—or better, with the several points of view of a human. But such identification cannot justify their being (posited) in the first place.

4.122   Though exiled within a parenthesis, the act of positing (positing as an act) is still playing a decisive role. It cannot be reduced to a *state* (of just being)—with all its associations of a coherent field to be quietly surveyed, at your leisure, changing nothing in it through the process. That functions are posited intimates rather that they are always competing with, and contradicting, one another, and are always at risk of being swallowed by the competition, of being denied. Nothing peaceful about it, nothing stagnant, nothing that can be (or worse, has been) settled once and for all. And again, this agonistic character extends to all other notions that (will be made to) depend on the positing of functions. Just as it itself derives from the generally agonistic, "political" nature of our metaphysics: that certain patterns are associated in a certain way is also a pattern, hence the competition among functions is but a special case of the competition among patterns. (And the positing of functions is "arbitrary" only for those who are taken in by the superficial, static picture sketched above. Though more must, and will, be said about this word.)

4.2   Given a set S of events and two abstractions T and U of S, U is *more expressive than* T if there are more (distinct) values for (distinct) members of S in U than there are in T.

4.21   It would be a lot of trouble to extend this notion to infinite sets (where the trouble may well be with set theory itself: it does make a lot of sense, after all, to say that there are more natural numbers than primes, but set theory is not able to do justice to that sense in any straightforward way). Here we remain largely unaffected by this issue, since infinite sets don't matter much for our concerns; so we might as well make all infinite abstractions maximally expressive (or, if you prefer, rank them according to where they stand in the transfinite hierarchy).

4.211   I can hear the rumbling as I say the above, and I can imagine the complaints as its significance sinks in in what follows. "What do you mean by languages being finite? Infinity is one of their most characteristic features!" So I must point out right away that this *is* a controversial view: that languages will be treated here as fragments of behavior, as bits and pieces casually thrown together, and that the ideal of a language as an inexhaustible, perfectly smooth mechanism will be considered a political (repressive) device. Inevitable, as every other twist and turn in our narrative, but still misleading (to the extent that it deviates from the origin, that it leads away from it and obfuscates it).

4.22   For example, all my moves could be mapped into a single interjection. Or they could be mapped into verbal descriptions of them. The latter mapping (abstraction) would be more expressive than the former.

4.221   But couldn't a simple "wow," uttered before a sunset, be *very* expressive—much more so, say, than a lengthy (literary?) description of the sunset? And aren't we doing unmotivated violence to the word "expressive" by refusing to take such phenomena into account? No, we are not: we are offering a framework in which the specific character of such phenomena can well be captured—better, indeed, than in any ordinary framework. For what is being mapped in these circumstances are (some of) the events constituting an experience, what they are mapped into are (some of) the events constituting another (possible) experience, and "wow" is the mapping. (Whereas, quite likely, a lengthy literary description of the sunset would only be mapping the experience of reading a certain literature into an inarticulate experience of self-satisfaction, and hence would be part of a process that is as little expressive as possible. The sunset, and the experience *of it*, would never even come into play.)

4.23   Any set is a maximally expressive abstraction of itself. But that abstraction is (in general) unlikely to have (or to maintain) enough strength to be posited, in view of its (general) uselessness. (There are exceptions, of course. Forms of life may become extremely stable, psychotically so, and [near?] perfect iteration may then be their only "expressive" strategy. Repetition, again—here with much less of a "saving" aura.)

4.24   Past a certain threshold, an abstraction will be called (simply) *expressive*.

4.241   Nothing is said here about the nature or location of the threshold.

4.3   Given an expressive abstraction S of a set T of (possible) events, a member a of S is an *anticipation* (at a time t) of a member *b* of its inverse image if (at *t*) *a* occurs while *b* has not occurred.

4.31   "Not occur" means "not be conspicuous, admitted as part of reality," which, of course, is perfectly compatible with (indeed, requires) being "real" in our more basic, "contradictory" sense. So *that* an event counts as an anticipation is the result of a play of forces—and might itself constitute a device for maintaining a certain equilibrium among those forces.

4.311   I might find myself anticipating events that have already been happening for a long time—that have indeed become a habit with me, except that they were never conspicuous. And it might well be that anticipating them has a lot to do with keeping them at that low level of visibility: that having them surface as purely hypothetical is precisely how I avoid recognizing them (consciously *or* unconsciously).

4.32   *b* might never occur. It might forever stay unreal. Anticipation has nothing necessarily to do with the real future. It has everything to do, however, with being *directed to* the future. *That is*, with what "the future" is first and foremost about, with its original (and often "forgotten") meaning.

4.33   What "the future" signifies, originally, is that reality is at stake, that the selection has not happened, that all competing patterns are viable options. Even the craziest, even the most frightful—especially the most frightful. (The future can only worry us; we can only be afraid of it.) Any attempt at "predicting" the future is one more attempt at conquering the manifold. At avoiding its impact; at denying the irruption of nonexistence it represents. (Don't confuse predicting the future with composing it, creating it. When you *make* the future, you face the opposition and acknowledge that there are alternatives to be overcome; when you *predict* it, alternatives are not assigned any dignity. And you have lost your dignity, too: what is predicted is simply *received*. Once more, courage is at stake.) Any success at such an attempt, any feeling that the future has been legislated, turned into a linear structure, that one can be reconciled with it *after all* (what a revealing expression!), robs our experience of its defining feature. It leaves us with the empty shell of an *empirical* (or again,

equivalently and ideologically, *real*) future, no longer worthy
of its name.

4.331   "Empirical" means "unquestioned": it points to the residue
of the questioning process (what was earlier called "contingent," as we were focusing on a different aspect of it—on
"there is no reason why it should be so," as opposed to "it
just is"). This is not to say that questions cannot be asked
about it; it is only to say that they are not (conspicuously).
When they are, the "empirical" is exploded. It becomes the
transcendental (or, in other words, the *logical*— "transcendental logic" is a revealing redundancy: it reveals that something is being done to logic, that logic is being shown to matter a lot more, to pervade "the world" much more intimately,
than one might [want to] think).

4.3311   So equating "empirical" and "real" means denying the reality
of questioning, of struggle, of the fundamental indeterminacy
and activity that lie within being. The empirical "data," indeed—being as something that is handed to me!

4.3312   But questioning can itself be flattened into the empirical,
turned into a cop-out. One might gloss the future by saying
that anything can happen and *thereby* reconcile oneself with
it. That the future is addressed transcendentally means that its
definition is open, *not* that its definition *is openness*.

4.3313   "Transcendental" and "original" come down to the same
thing because, to begin with, everything is up for grabs.

4.332   We know that it's no different with the past. The past too is
nonlinear, and is forced into a linear mold. Turned into a
wasteland, a cemetery, a *fact:* "what is done cannot be un-
done." (And predicting the future amounts to reducing it to
this past. "The future will resemble the past." Remember
what "predictable" meant for us: "such as has *already* happened.") Though it will sometimes react successfully against
this violence, and surprise you, and reveal its enormous potential. And though locally its very colonization may be turned
against the colonizers: show them undeniable evidence of conflict, force them to admit that conflict itself is a fact that is not
going to go away, be signed off by a treaty—treaties are part

of it. With the future, however, the forcing encounters more opposition: it is more immediately vivid, harder to deny, that *what the future is* is in question. We are not so willing to give that up. We are more attached to what we are *not yet;* we feel more strongly that that's exactly what we *are,* that depriving us of it is depriving us of our being.

4.3321   Don't blame this robbery too quickly on "science." And don't feel relieved too quickly when science "goes indeterministic." Science may be the main opportunity for freedom that is left to us: its (alleged) goal of predicting the future is the main excuse socially available for following up the most absurd dreams—and sometimes making them real, making them our *present.* Though, of course, politicians are not to be told that, nor are their agents in the labs: the bureaucrats who are out to close this opportunity, to turn freedom into the slavery of adding meaningless numbers and writing useless grant applications. They are the real enemies, not "determinism," which traditionally has been a very valuable ally. (What a grand, superb, inspiring mirage a Laplacean universe is! How it gets the juices flowing, the brain storming!) Whatever the current theory—the current excuse for play—the same confrontation will be staged between experimentation and administration.

4.33211   Think of the viciousness of throwing an "anything goes" at scientists. Of how it might dampen their enthusiasm, kill their morale. Make them stare emptily at useless battles, start wondering whether perhaps a buck couldn't be made.

4.4   A series of events that anticipate all members of a pattern constitute an anticipation of that pattern.

4.41   The relation of anticipation between two patterns is not injective. As with abstractions in general, distinct elements in a pattern may be related to a single element in the other one.

4.42   Remember the risk element in all this. The very same sequence of events might or might not be an anticipation, and whether or not it is cannot simply be "decided" once. That it is an anticipation depends on a positing, and such positing is constantly, essentially threatened. It is constantly, essentially possible for a sequence of events to be just that—a sequence of events. To be opaque, meaningless, to be *what it is.* I am not speaking about what is not, you will say (and how could I, since there is nothing that is not?); I am not expectant or afraid of the future (since, again, the future *is not*). I am just moving my tongue and producing articulated sounds. And shivering, perhaps, I am not sure why. (I must be cold, I must have gotten the flu, I must . . . , I must . . .)

4.5   An anticipation of a violation of an entrenched pattern is an anticipated violation of that pattern.

4.51   Anticipated violations of patterns are themselves patterns— on a par, "theoretically," with any others. Don't make too much of their "fictitious" character, or you would be denying them what impact they can have, despite their (comparative) weakness: denying how much they can help (themselves and others). You must be constantly watching for the kind of disrespect that breeds obliteration.

4.511   "We must remember, or the Holocaust will happen again."

4.512   Remember with passion, with commitment, with urgency: remember something (as much as possible) as real. To do it justice: to make room for it, to let it be, to resist one's greed.

4.513   Remember *so that* justice can be done—or injustice cannot. "Examples" like these begin to suggest that repetition in memory can be an alternative to real repetition, that the former can serve to exorcise the latter. That the real commitment to it (commitment to it *as* real) might prevent us from being committed to it in reality. (But, of course, these are no mere examples, insofar as we are talking about evil *itself,* about the Platonic idea of what must be exorcised. So there is a sense in which every other case of exorcism will turn out to be an "example" of this one.) We begin to see how language originates in magic: in the ritualistic conjuring up (mimicking) of events one is trying to chase away. To get the full significance of this origin, we need to expand our view (of what is being chased) from the past to the future.

4.6   Anticipated violations of patterns may be less painful than the violations themselves.

4.61 The child in *Beyond the Pleasure Principle* suffers less by playing the "Fort"/"Da" game than by having his mother leaving and returning. But that is not all there is to it. Indeed, it's not even the most important part.

4.7 An anticipated violation of a pattern may also reduce the pain associated with the violation itself, when the latter occurs. If it does, it's called *efficient*.

4.71 It may reduce the component of the pain associated with the violation just being a violation ("I've been there before; I know what it's like"—we'll say a few nasty things about that in a minute); and it may reduce any other pain (deriving from undesirable consequences of the violation), based on the familiarity with the new context vicariously achieved through its anticipation.

4.711 The first time I am out at sea I may find the whole thing less scary because of how many stories about it I told myself (or read), and I may also avoid being hit by the steering wheel because of how many times I was "hit" by it in those stories— and how eventually I thus "learned" to "handle it."

4.712 "Familiarity with the new context" is a misleading expression: those familiar and those unfamiliar with "one and the same context" are actually in *very different* contexts, so familiarity with a context *changes* it. This is a crucial point, and will come up again.

4.72 But there is no guarantee of it; it all depends on how much familiarity is in fact achieved (how much we have changed the context).

4.721 In my stories I may have spent too much time watching the sunset or making love to the native girls, and too little learning to handle the steering wheel. Or my mapping of the steering wheel may have been very *very* sketchy. And I may live to regret it. I may never get to "really" watch the sunset because I didn't play enough "in thought" (we don't yet know what thought is) with the steering wheel.

4.7211 On the other hand, though storytelling might teach me nothing useful about sailing (make me acquire no valuable familiarity with it), it will probably teach me a whole lot about *telling stories about sailing* (make me familiar with *that*). And this other teaching may turn out to be quite useful to me. The world may be such that being good at storytelling is a much more bankable commodity than being good at sailing.

4.722   Hail fell unexpectedly on the Dallas airport on April 29, 1995, causing millions of dollars in damage. Meanwhile, a computer program in Norman, Oklahoma, designed to mimic the behavior of the atmosphere, was tracking the same group of storms and anticipating their behavior. Except that it anticipated it two counties off. The problem: "data sparsity." *Our* problem: *how much* data is going to be enough? (And enough for what?)

4.7221   You know how it's done: to begin with, you don't know what you need. So you start somewhere, and if it doesn't work you keep adding stuff, until it works better. As it does, you come to believe more and more that you "understand" the process—that you have the right "picture" of it. Though, of course, you never have a picture *of it*—or always do: pictures can be very badly drawn. Well, what you need to do now is start thinking of what goes on in your "mind" the same way.

4.73   When not enough familiarity is achieved, and the same undesirable consequences follow, they are often tempered by the idle smile of those who "could see it coming" and can tell (themselves?): "See, I told you so." They are still getting something out of their anticipatory work; they can *say* that that was not a violation (it didn't violate their expectations)—though, of course, they are still suffering from it (it still *is* a violation). The irony of it is how deluded—and badly off—ironists are. How theirs is a mere simulacrum of control: control turned into an irrepressible, exhausted tic (into sheer, obtuse sociability with their discomfort).

4.74   The advantageous consequences of familiarity constitute the cash value of the claim that theories can be "informative" about practices (and, in general, about matters of fact).

4.741   Theory construction and manipulation is also a practice, which may end up "infecting" other practices: making new patterns conspicuous (that outcome is called "mutation") which are credible competitors, which must be reckoned with, with which compromises must be reached. (Think of the genetic "pattern" of a virus that has issued from laboratory work; think of it spreading outside the lab.) Also, a pattern that does not have enough strength to make it (yet) all the way to reality may sojourn indefinitely in this neutral make-believe area—and thereby possibly gather the strength it needs for that momentous step.

4.742   Though whether it ever will, or how long it will take before it does, cannot be decided in advance. Individual cases will have to find their individual, a posteriori resolution. (Again, saying so amounts to accepting the future for what it is, remaining open to it—in a state of listening, of concernful attention. You can—indeed, you must—be in that state toward yourself, too: always affectionately ready to learn more from your own moves, to revise your self-description accordingly, unwilling to brutally submit your complexity to a barren, rudimentary set of preconceived "intentions.")

4.7421 ("I am going to write it down, to find out what I think.")

4.7422 Does riding a motorcycle help when you eventually get behind the wheel of a car? Does riding a horse? A toy car? Does watching others drive? Reading or being told about driving? Thinking about it—about how it would go? (Again, we don't yet know what thinking is.) These questions will be answered differently relative to different people, depending on their capacity for aping—on their "imagination."

4.74221 The most human of skills, the power of calling up what is not (present), is substantiated by the most apelike behavior: it gets "realized" through patient, humble imitation (possibly, indeed often, of oneself—of some other "oneself") and through the painstaking, intrinsically illegitimate expansion of learned routines to new contexts—contexts for which those routines were not originally "intended." And I am talking about physical routines, involving hands and feet and (sometimes) mouth: about how I have seen a certain clearing of one's throat, a certain furrowing of one's eyebrows, a certain curious inflection, "migrate" from one person to another. (Often

I could tell that two people had met without ever seeing them together.) In the case of utterances, I am talking about the (modalities of the) uttering, not about its content. *And* I am talking about the possibility that (just as "the same" clearing of someone's throat can be reproduced by someone else, or "the same" finger movement can migrate from a typewriter to a computer keyboard) "the same" pattern of utterances be reproduced as a pattern of nonutterances, and someone's nonverbal behavior be invaded by structures that originated in a verbal medium. When that happens—when something that began as verbal activity issues in a constellation of physical moves—people will often say that they *found* the content of the verbalization to be true (that it was true all along, and they just found out about it), but all such talk is delusive (in the same way in which the expression "familiarity with the new context" is misleading): what's really going on is that their practices are now different and those different practices started out small, with an experimental verbal "copy" of them—or rather with something that will turn out to *have been* a copy after the experiment proves successful, largely *because of* this success. So don't think of a theory finding application in reality but rather of the "application" changing the moves reality consists of, and of the change being initiated in a linguistic lab. Think of theorizing as a way of appropriating deviance and playing it out, and of this being a process by which often deviance appropriates the world.

4.74222   One might be able to check this expansion to new contexts against the "original," and as a result get gradually more confident about what one is doing. Though this confidence is no guarantee that one is not getting it "wrong." And though, in the end, it doesn't much matter. On the contrary, it is in survival's best interest if time and again this sort of thing is done *slightly* wrong. That's what makes mutation possible, and a large part of what makes imagination *productive*. (The other part, which is usually regarded as merely *re*productive, is the decontextualization process itself. But, of course, the two are strictly related; after all, decontextualizing is already altering to some extent.)

4.74223   We get angry when "the right" challenges our relationship to apes, but we are hardly making this relationship a respectable intellectual issue. We pay lip service to "evolution" and then continue to reason according to creationist models. Models by which being-human (the set of moves, of practices that being-human consists of) is not just a sophisticated, stratified, complexified form of aping; in which instead an incomprehensible, unresolvable, highly dignified chasm exists between us and "our nearest cousins." There will be no real continuity as long as distinct kinds of explanation are used.

4.74224   We need to give gorillas and chimps their philosophical due. Bring them out of the closet where we hid them (out of embarrassment and anxiety). Give them at least as much credit as we give dogs (and computers).

4.74225   But, you will say, how can I at the same time assign as much foundational value to narratives as I do *and* reduce the uttering of stories to "blind," apelike mimicry? A silly question, and also, because of that, an extremely useful one. It presupposes the very anthropocentrism I am denying: it collapses "stories" into "human stories," stories a human could tell (and understand). It reduces the metaphysical stance defended here to the most trivial "empirical idealism." Whereas the significance of placing stories at the core of being, and the monstrous challenge evoked by that move (monstrous like a chimp's grin: it's your own face that is being distorted), consists precisely in setting the (impossible) task of thinking *nonhuman* stories: stories apes tell with their hands and electrons with their spins. And of rethinking human stories in such a way that what is essential about them is what they share with nonhuman ones.

4.74226   Ultimately, then, the context in which we place this discussion of mimicry is the metaphysical primacy of patterns over "things": their "will" to duplicate themselves indefinitely, hence their capacity to grab different media for such duplication. What happens when "the same" expression stamps a new face, for us, is that that particular expression has had enough strength (sustained, probably, by an underlying emotional current connecting the owners of the relevant faces) to extend its area of influence a bit farther. (Not that this formulation really makes anyone understand anything: one will probably know what the words mean, but it's quite another matter to see it that way.)

4.74227 (As a step toward developing that kind of vision, consider the following question/objection: What is the difference between saying that we have hit upon the right theory of a storm's behavior and saying that the storm's behavior has the same pattern as our computer simulation? Answer: Once you put it that way, the difference is largely gone; but that is because your formulation is already committed to the traditional view. For us, there is no such thing as *the* pattern of the storm's behavior—or of the computer simulation. Remember the primacy of multiplicity: indefinitely many distinct and conflicting patterns apply with equal legitimacy to [any portion of] the manifold—*are* with equal legitimacy [that portion of] the manifold—and they constantly compete for conspicuousness. Resonance at different locations [say, the storm and the computer] is a crucial element in determining [a temporary] success in this competition; and success will mean that what else the storm's behavior is [including anything other than *a storm's* behavior] is forced underground [into unreality], where it may remain indefinitely long. But that is all there is to a "correct" anticipation: no "carving of Nature at its joints" or any such nonsense.)

4.743   A major practical effect of theory construction and manipulation is to give more weight to theories—and theorizers.

4.7431   Saying that the world is a text might make texts more prominent. Or saying that one will better master something if he has access to its *idea* (or to an accurate description of it) might empower those who ideate (or describe). Alternative tactics for defending the same privilege. Sometimes viciously opposed to one another. Nothing like a little tempest in a teacup to make sure you will continue to enjoy tea (and those others will continue to serve it).

4.7432   When people who are good at wordplay succeed in making wordplay "the thing," they will congratulate themselves for it—for how smart they are. Which, in a (lurid) way, is indeed the case.

4.8 So anticipated violations are "ultimately" in the interest of the real.

4.81 They would not be possible otherwise. It would not be possible for them to be real (*as* anticipations). And for the (possible) future to become real through them—however far that process is allowed to go.

4.811 No one would be funding the think tanks, the researchers, the scholars. The lackeys.

4.812 Who knows? We put a little money into the RAND Corporation and we might even win the cold war. A side bet, which we can afford since we have plenty of bread and butter. Of guns, too—in case things get out of hand.

4.82 But still, they *are* possible.

4.83 And, however diligently working for the status quo, they are still working after their own fashion. Hence, perhaps, still making trouble.

4.831 The lackeys might kill you. Indeed, they probably will. (It's always the godfather's bodyguard—or the Roman emperor's, or the English king's—who ends up doing him in.)

4.832 You might "win" the cold war and suddenly lose all your power and national identity. And forever wonder how it could happen, in the midst of such great fortune. You did not see *that one* coming! (And are not laughing about it.)

4.833 But *I* do (?!).

4.9 However useful "in the long run" (and however minimal their impact, as compared with "the real thing"), anticipated violations still hurt. They are sadistic practices, not at all redeemed by having the practitioner (often) suffer the most. Being "on the side" of transgression, even when the transgression is mediated through "symbols," is being on the side of pain, of that breaking down of integrated tissues and organs which causes pain.

4.91 And there is no denying that "I" am on the side of transgression (do "I" have a choice? and am *I* the subject of the previous question?). There is no denying the cruelty of all of this.

Other than by just, unapologetically, *denying* it, that is, calling it a pretense, "academic." (If you want to know what's really going on in academia, think of Konrad Lorenz's caged doves.) Exonerating the executioners by turning them into clowns. Which shows what's so scary about clowns.

4.92   What, then, about the banality of evil? Is there a justification for the recurring attacks against thoughtlessness? Yes, there is: we have already suggested that playing things out in thought *may* help avoid doing them for real. One might vicariously "experience" horror and regret, and *use* those sentiments to abstain from "true" violence. But don't go to sleep on this; don't take it as the end of the story. There is no end to it: there is only the necessity of constant vigilance. Once you create a "harmless," protective environment for the nurturing of horrifying nightmares, *those nightmares will be nurtured,* and it will always be possible for them to spread outside the lab where you are trying to have it both ways (and maybe, for a while, are succeeding—which remote possibility accounts for the few, *brief* "Renaissances" of humankind, *and* for their being steeped in blood).

4.93   Education to freedom is a supremely important tool, and a duty—necessary insofar as humanity is defined by reference to freedom (all necessity is based on a definition, and on the choice of it: on the decision to establish a certain constitutive connection, to build and maintain a certain bridge). But educators should be aware of the fire they are playing with. They should still play with it, of course, but expect no blanket reassurance that they are doing "the right thing." No comforting pat on the back, no absolution. They, too, owe it to themselves and others not to be cowardly. No education is possible without risk taking; none occurs unless one is prepared to bet on a future one will not live to see.

4.931   Is indoctrination education? Is advertising? Yes: though the bet and the risk are not subjectively felt, they are still present. (Nor, for that matter, are they subjectively felt, usually, within an education to freedom. One usually needs to—and does— tell oneself various deceptive, edifying stories. Make it sound as if one knew a lot about how it will turn out—whereas of course one doesn't.) Indeed, there may be more risk and more at stake there. Making people respond very predictably means making them very stiff, and consequently very fragile. The whole thing might blow up in your face before you have a chance to cash in. (Though, if you do cash in, it might be a nice payoff—assuming you live long enough to spend it.) And it *will* blow up, eventually. You are setting a time bomb: that's the future you (hope you) will not live to see. And, at some level, you are afraid of it.

5   A language is an expressive abstraction (of *some* set S) that makes possible efficient anticipated violations of patterns.

5.1   Not every (expressive) abstraction counts as a language. Bodily moves might be mapped into other bodily moves with no significant advantage in terms of diminishing pain (say, certain forms of torture could be mapped into other, equally agonizing forms of torture). A language must offer means of staving off undesirable events (such as undesirable consequences of one's actions).

5.11   We don't want to reduce language to homomorphisms in general—not even to those which are "expressive," or *posited*. There is an emotional, caring aspect to language, a way for it to matter for us, to be protective and joyful, *and also, because of that,* to (occasionally) hurt; this element we intend to capture through the notion of efficiency.

5.111   Think of people sitting around a fire at night, talking about the hardship of the day (and thus making for less hardship tomorrow). Laughing, too: finding consolation and relief in the verbal familiarity they acquire with their misery (and the learning that follows from it). And think of a pearl generated by the intrusion of an irritating particle: of how its beauty could not arise without an initial discomfort. (There is a lot about language that is just as beautiful: words are precious, enchanting gifts. Hence they are also dangerous, like all gifts.) What is insulting and demeaning about the algebraic notion of language is that it misses this element—this protectiveness and creativity.

5.12   Turning language into an algebra is not only a misunderstanding (is there *any* such?). Some definite interests are expressed thereby—not the ones endorsed here, for sure. (Once the caring element is gone from language, who is going to still care for it? Perfect emotional stillness will bring about its demise.)

5.121   Be careful not to read this position as, again, anthropocentric. I am *not* saying that, because only humans (or, maybe, higher animals) care, only humans can have a language. There is care (and strength, and struggle) anywhere in being; when you define language as an algebra, you are not reducing the human to the nonhuman—you are dismissing vital aspects of the human and the nonhuman alike. Your ravishment of humanity is the natural climax of a general ravishment of being.

5.1211   Are you shocked by the thought that electrons might care for their environment (and vice versa)? I am, too: I too have been brainwashed into thinking that the care structure identifies only a certain kind of being. Which, once you believe it, makes it so much easier not to care for whatever we have decided does *not* have that kind of being. (It will be different things at different times, of course; but the root of the problem is the very existence of such a radical distinction.)

5.13   Exactly what condition is expressed by requiring that a language make efficient anticipated violations of patterns *possible*? We don't want to say that such anticipations must occur *sometimes* (read possibility à la Diodorus Cronus), since we want to allow for languages that though they *could* work that way, never quite do, for "contingent" "empirical" reasons. And, conversely, we don't want to stretch this notion of possibility too thin and have it become trivial. Our position will consist of emphasizing once more the narrative element. The claim that a given abstraction is a language must be supported by a story: an account of how it is *necessarily* possible that efficient anticipations issue from that abstraction. This story (this *pattern*) will compete with all alternatives, using what strength it has; and the competition will have one of the usual outcomes. The story might be defeated outright, and hence not "surface" at all; or win handily; or do neither, thus making the relevant language available *but also* open to question (about its character *as* a language). Depending on the outcome, the story will or will not substantiate the "possibility" involved in our definition, and consequently sanction the associated claim.

5.131   But then couldn't any homomorphism be characterized by an appropriate story as an efficient way of dealing with pain? Yes, of course: we are not interested in ruling out certain specific abstractions as languages but rather in ruling out a certain conception of what *makes* them languages. And, therefore, in setting a corresponding task for anyone who wants to decide whether something is or is not a language—a task the opposite conception would regard as irrelevant. (We are not competing with algebras but with other philosophies of language. And, of course, an algebra is never *just* an algebra— for some, it may even be a love object.)

5.1311   (I may desire infinity with a passion. It may even be that anything I desire with a passion is infinite. Which is probably what I mean when I say that my language is infinite. Though, of course, saying it doesn't make it so. Not right away. Not as long as I still need to say it—as long as I still care. As long as that is still a language.)

5.1312   Making it sound as if something can always be done is often a main strategy for convincing people never to do it. For the strategy to be successful, it has to shrewdly downplay the effort and ingenuity involved in realizing that possibility—reduce it from a real to a logical possibility.

5.132   An objection: isn't it circular, or an infinite regress, to refer to stories in making sense of the "possible" included in the definition of a language? No more than is circular, or an infinite regress, to use quantification theory in proving the soundness and completeness of quantification theory. The distinction between language and metalanguage obscures the issue: what one is doing in both cases is entering an interconnected system at some point or other, and traveling within it, and hitting the same elements of it from different angles, and going through this exercise long enough to gain some confidence that that *is* a system—that it holds together. The procedure (in both cases) is indeed circular, and could indeed go on forever, and there is nothing wrong with any of that.

5.2 Language is not necessarily associated with sounds. I may anticipate patterns efficiently by dancing. By playing a board game. By plotting figures on a screen.

5.21 This is not to say, however, that sounds "don't matter," or are "purely accidental" manifestations of language: they represent the best compromise available between a very rich and articulate structure (which is also true, say, of visual patterns) and one that has a chance for maximal impact (which is also true, say, of smells)—you don't have to pay attention to sounds (or smells), don't have to consider them (or, at least, where they are coming from) interesting to begin with, to be affected by them. So they are the best medium at our disposal for having nonbeing work at being, "thought" bring about "action." As such, they will surface again in what follows.

5.22 Computers will make us all dumb. Not because they will force silence on us, but because there will no longer be any point to speaking. (The two activities compete for control of the same ecological niche.) Eventually, we will grow weary of talk, and do it sluggishly. We will lose any facility with it. And any pleasure it might have given us.

5.221 There may be a point then for Language Fitness Centers, where to exercise with spoken words for an hour a day. We will need speech therapists to tell us how to utter sentences and paragraphs—after forgetting all about it. (And it won't work, of course: an hour a day is never going to be enough, if nothing else helps. It will be like going to the symphony after dinner, with coarse food still stuck between your teeth. Or like going to school and then coming home to the soaps.)

5.23 Our form of life will end all too sweetly. And that's unfortunate, as there will be no heroes to this tragedy—as indeed it will not be a tragedy at all. There will be no warfare, no anguish, no sacrifice.

5.231 Why is that unfortunate? Because then the end will not "really" have happened. Nothing will have happened. Nothing will simply (gradually) take over.

5.232   And yet that might not be a problem, from a certain angle. Nothing's angle, precisely: the angle of what is not. This development might turn out to be the supreme form of transgression, of subversion of what is, and it looks as if "I" should like it. But I don't. Which suggests that *I* am not "I"—or not only that, not only my origin. I have come to terms with that origin, to very specific, *confrontational* terms. I am speaking from a definite (and somewhat hostile: hostile to *some whats*) place in the process I am speaking of.

5.233   I espouse a form of "humanism." I favor (continuing) the appropriation of deviance by humans: (continuing) the enforcement of a certain definition. I consider an enemy any position that speaks in the name of different life-forms: networks, states, churches, gods. Even when "speaking in the name" of such enemies is sold as just a description of "how things are (and will be)," urging us all "not to remain behind." There is nothing necessarily valuable about going with the flow, however irresistible the flow might (be conceived to) be—unless you take the flow's own point of view, or maybe the point of view of its next station. There may be a lot that is valuable (from where you are sitting) about sticking your finger in the dike, to delay its collapse by even a split second.

5.234   Can I say this after denouncing anthropocentrism as much as I did? Yes: I am trying to fight fair and square (courage matters to me). I acknowledge my enemy's dignity, which is (in principle—independently of any successful "empirical" encroaching) the same as my own; I don't avoid recognition of the fierceness of our conflict by cheap metaphysical tricks. The anthropocentrism I have denounced, and will continue to denounce, is the "theoretical" variety—which is also (what a perverse, symptomatic twisting of words!) the *blind* variety.

5.2341   Not being blind entails a greater deal of suffering. For one can then *see* the equal legitimacy of other positions, and occasionally be strongly attracted by them—grabbed by the relevant patterns. I chose my examples carefully above (drawing a pattern favorable to my goals): networks, states, churches, and gods (especially if cited quickly, in one and the same breath) are not going to generate a lot of sympathy among the people inclined to read this text. But what about "thinking like a mountain"? Isn't that something I feel there ought to be room for? Indeed it is; so my practical anthropocentrism issues in sin. And I am aware of that sin, and will try to integrate concrete cases of "thinking like a mountain" as much as possible within an anthropological project, and hope that I forever have the "moral luck" not to face a really hard case. (Consider *Sophie's Choice,* if you want to know what I mean by that—and if you are a parent.) Because I know what I would choose then, and I know that it would be wrong. And I must live with that—better, cohabitation with that *is* my life, it defines *my* position in this narrative.

5.235   Note also that one is not "always already" human. Humanity should not be understood as automatically including bodies of a certain shape; "humanity" should not be used in a lazy "referential" way. Humanity is indeed a project: the project of making certain bodies temples of diversity. So, if I favor (and I do) certain bodies, I favor their *becoming* human (their becoming what they are), their struggling to conquer and maintain humanity, to justify the definition I want to be true of them. I favor the disciplined, painstaking effort of building enough structure so that deviance can happen inside those bodies without taking them apart; ultimately, I favor the *constitution* of a human self—as an arena for a transgression that is not purely negative (destructive) of that very self.

5.2351   There are two possible alternatives to this position. One is to defend the appropriation of deviance by some other kind of body. And then there is the shifty, deceptive defense of undifferentiated freedom, of freedom "pure," which does not want to appreciate the necessity of a background and a framework for freedom (and deviance) to have any content. And often ends up being used, at crucial moments in history, as a ploy for instituting new forms of domination—without ever admitting to it.

5.2352   Or for eventually reasserting traditional forms of domination while providing worthless fodder to the rage of the populace—and thus defusing it, by *con*fusing it. "If we want things to stay as they are, things will have to change" (Tomasi di Lampedusa, *The Leopard*).

5.236 Let me be clearer about it, because what I am saying is not pretty, and I don't want it to sound as if it were. Favoring certain bodies, bodies of a certain kind, with a certain structure—ultimately, bodies that look enough like mine—is a totally arbitrary position. I can imagine myself (no, not quite myself, but somebody who reasons in the same way) leaving out of this class, say, black bodies, or women's bodies, or Jewish ones. As much as I can imagine such a person wanting to include roaches and ants (and networks and states and churches and gods). And I am not saying that there will not be an enormous amount of rationalizing that goes into making this choice; but I am saying that the rationalizing by itself won't do, and that somehow the person who makes the choice knows it. Which is the best I can say about him (about me): if he's not fooled by the rationalization, he will have to make more of a constant expenditure to maintain his position, and as a consequence probably exhaust his resources sooner, and last less. And thus give everybody else more of a chance.

5.3   A language is intrinsically private.

5.31   My *pain* is *my* pain: unless there is a structure that is broken down, there is no pain—and then the pain is *that structure's*. And a language is one way *I* deal with it (often, before it happens—or, so that it might never happen).

5.32   This is a costly and delicate way of dealing with pain: an indirect, long-range approach that pays no immediate dividends. What makes it feasible is a repressive move: the isolation of difference, its being deprived of access. Which has the effect of turning it (for a while, at least) into a formidable weapon.

5.321 There is an outside "within" myself, a multiplicity that I can use to articulate "objective" perspectives on my "internal" behavior.

5.3211 That multiplicity of perspectives is the origin of consciousness. Not Consciousness capitalized yet, not my "official" self (that will surface later in the narrative), but rather the capacity for an ironic look, for estranged contemplation. This capacity allows for a lot of decontextualization, of (productive and reproductive) imagination, of aping and infecting, to go on "inside." For a lot of what we might call internal *dialogue* or *play:* an activity that is quite useful to the structure I am. Its value is most apparent when one of my entrenched routines is violated and my various "souls," seeing the crisis as an opening, proceed to fight it out—until perhaps one of them, or some compromise among them, is able to handle the trouble successfully. But such "productive exchanges" would not occur if the same activity were not going on (less conspicuously) at all times.

5.322   Indeed, that outsideness *is* myself: it is what sets a *self* (or a *subject*) in contrast with an *object* (if indeed there are any of the latter—which is a serious issue).

5.3221   And therefore it makes sense to identify my self with my consciousness. Except that what is ordinarily meant by that identification is substantially different from what is understood here (and, again, we have to wait until later to make complete sense of this).

5.3222   That's where multiplicity has been exiled. Objects are as much "different from themselves" as subjects are, *to begin with.* Then they are made "real" (their superpositional character becomes "unintelligible"), and difference becomes a private thing—something that goes on in the backyard, away from indiscreet looks, for the benefit (possibly) of the house owners.

5.32221   Of course, I also look like an object from the outside (it is on this basis that most other people interact with me). So I must admit that all objects could also be selves from the inside— that most of them probably are. (All those which have not been totally stilled, completely digested by some other pattern ["treat others never simply as means, but always at the same time as ends"—or, the essence of morality].)

5.3223   But this exile may be what gives multiplicity its best chance. It helps to have thick walls protecting the play going on inside, for then the play *can happen*—it's not wiped out by thermodynamic death. Those walls are (largely) behavioral structures, solid routines implanted by long, tiresome discipline and practice. Nobody is freer than someone who can stand on his own feet and take care of himself. Nobody is more frightening also, looked at with more suspicion—a good indication that others sense the revolutionary potential of independence. They sense that independent-*minded*ness begins with independence period, with self-sufficiency and self-containment. You should take Stoics seriously.

5.3224   So (to rehearse another old line) nothing is more destructive of freedom than license. A good example: how to destroy the creativity of promising young filmmakers by throwing lots of money at them. Contra the dominant historical tendency, intellectuals ought not to become whores. Far better for them to be civil servants instead—though it will not help if they get swallowed by their public role, if they don't use the opportunity it gives them. (What else would you expect a—pained—civil servant to say? See how patterns strive to maintain themselves?)

5.3225   Note also that this diligent practical learning does more than just create an environment favorable to the occurrence of internal play. For that play takes place by having several characters (personalities) engage one another (care about conquering one another to their respective patterns—which ends up [as dialogue ordinarily does] making all develop their own distinct identities further, as each finds ever more ingenious ways of resisting the challenges the others make to its integrity), and hence is more creative the more detailed those characters (the more developed, and hence resourceful, their identities) are to begin with. Therefore, after equipping yourself with a consistent set of routines as a prerequisite for the possibility of play, if you now want play to become actual, you must simply be equipping "yourself" with more such consistent sets. Which, of course, demands even more discipline and exercise, even more painstaking work.

5.3226   Don't listen to the sirens who tell you to let go, to let it happen, to follow what comes naturally. Your nature must first be educated to recognize the value of toil, so that toil *will* come naturally, so that you will even miss it. You need to acquire a *second* nature, and then a third . . .

5.32261   A multiple personality "disorder" is where this structure shows up most clearly. What is missing from it is the ideological unification brought about by Consciousness capitalized, and that's what makes this purest example of subjectivity a "disorder." Once again, pathologizing as a main strategy for maintaining a position of power.

5.3227   Along these lines, I might even convince myself that while I am working in favor of a specifically human structure, I am also working in favor of transgression and liberation — of *real* transgression and liberation, as opposed to the self-destructive, vacuous, dissipative kind. But that argument would be too quick, and biased. It may be in the eventual best interest of transgression that it be conducted within some solid structure (that way, transgression lasts longer, if indeed that is *its* best interest — what is surfacing here is a compromise between two sets of values, those of transgression and those of survival, so that we end up valuing *the survival of transgression*), but no reason has been given (nor can I think of one) why that structure should be a human one.

5.3228   Also, along these lines I can understand the different pronouns used as grammatical subjects in this book. There is "you": any interlocutor in the dialogue that subjectivity is, and that acts out ("produces") the book. There is "one" (or, sometimes, "they," or even, when it's not conceived as a person, "it"): any element of that dialogue when it's not being addressed, when it's not engaged in an argument but looked at from the outside, "objectively," often unsympathetically. There is "we": the temporary consensus strenuously worked out within this plurality, and ready to break down at any moment, as "you" come up with an objection or "one"'s position is found to be shaky. And, finally, there is "I": the grammatical structure that identifies the "narrator" with the "actor," thereby making dialogue and multiplicity relevant to "the world" and posing the challenge of articulating them "empirically" (there is now an empirical world to a large extent—

reality has been largely fixated—and "I", must find a way of relating to it, the subject/dialogue must also be part of that world, identical with one of the "things" in it). *I* (the "empirical I") am a specific (temporary, unsatisfactory, revisable) outcome in the enterprise of facing this challenging task, constantly under pressure from the task itself, constantly called in question by that signature "I" which represents the task "transcendentally."

5.323   Therefore, that language is essentially private does not immediately make it a soliloquy but rather its opposite. Only afterward does this private language become monologic, as repression gets more thorough and invasive. The self is increasingly denied opportunities for developing difference, or the endurance needed to sustain it—and its conversation comes to an end.

5.324   You are stuck with listening to the grumblings of "your" stomach, to your itchings and your erections, told to identify with them and nothing else. Isolation is not safe enough; it's not enough to keep you under lock and key, disconnected from any immediate resonance your din might have in the public arena. You must also wear a straitjacket, and be blindfolded, and gagged. *That* is now called privacy.

5.325   Then comes the ultimate insult: the notion of a private language is inconsistent, it will not bear conceptual pressure. You mean I can't speak after everyone has left, and my tongue has been glued to my palate?

5.326   None of this should be confused with *thought,* that is (finally!), with the lively dialogue that occurs inside the subject when the latter is not (yet?) incapacitated. There is no silence to thought: there is constant arguing and screaming, though, of course, "the public" does not hear it. So "refutations" of private language confuse this rich, powerful exchange with the dejected solitude that results from banning it, and that confusion is a main tactic for enforcing the ban. (We, on the other hand, see thought as the destiny of language: language is still available to the public, whereas thought is clearly owned by the structure to which it—and language—belonged in the first place.)

5.4   An *articulated* language establishes equivalence relations
          among the events it is an abstraction of, determines the rele-
          vant equivalence classes, and divides them into categories.
          And it contains elements corresponding to those classes (as
          well as to their elements).

5.41   *Thing* and *attribute* have traditionally been the most success-
          ful categories.

5.411   That they are such an uneasy match for the "underlying"
          metaphysical structure is no problem. On the contrary, the re-
          sulting "torsion" is welcome: a language would be useless if it
          did not modify what it allegedly *re*-presents. (Who, aside
          from psychotics and their counterparts in philosophy depart-
          ments, needs patterns to be duplicated indefinitely?)

5.4111   (Making philosophy representational is a good way of wast-
          ing time—and maintaining the hold of reality. For how much
          is there to represent! It will never be done! The encyclopedia
          will take forever, and prevent us from doing anything else.
          Except for the redeeming power of *imperfect* repetition.)

5.42   In an articulated language, it is possible to identify common
          components of various events and break down the mapping
          of those events into a mapping of the components. This strat-
          egy is more economical than just mapping events into unana-
          lyzed linguistic events. And, because it is more economical, it
          is also likely to be more expressive and more efficient (better
          at protecting from pain). So the pressure is on to develop lan-
          guages in this direction (indeed, to make the process an iter-
          ated one).

5.5   An element of a language *refers* to any element of its inverse
          image.

5.51   In an articulated language, some elements refer to events,
          some to equivalence classes of events, some to equivalence
          classes of these equivalence classes, and so on.

5.52   And, in such a language (because of the torsion mentioned
          above), simplicity is often a misleading indicator. For exam-
          ple, simple sounds may refer to complex entities, and vice versa.

5.521   "That at time t I uttered a cry" refers, in the ontology we adopted, to a simple (an event—but remember: this simplicity is not immediate, not primordial; it is itself the result of hard labor, not accounted for here), whereas "cry" refers to a complex (that is, to something *yet more* complex).

6   A language is duplicitous.

6.1   Abstractions are events, *and* they are correlated with (other) events.

6.2   What makes a language *a language* is the correlation, and the protection it affords from (the pain associated with) the correlated events. But the events the language is made of also fall into patterns, and these patterns may become entrenched, and become integrated in larger (entrenched) patterns.

6.21   Soon language is conquered by the public sphere.

6.211   That is, by the real. Real *is* public. Which statement "says" opposite things at different times in our story. Initially, it brings out the character of multiplicity in the messy, fuzzy manifold that *original* reality is. But then the "ones" are able to convert that manifold into a *community*. Into a form of life, into *uni*formity. And then the statement expresses the triumph of their ideology: the public sphere becomes ("in reality") what successfully counteracts multiplicity.

6.212   When I say "Slab!" and you bring me a slab, our behavior is governed by an entrenched pattern, just as much as it would be if you brought me a slab whenever (and as soon as) you could see that I am out of slabs. Language turns into a quick, efficient way "to get the job done." (Which, ironically, it could not be if it were not "efficient" in its primordial sense— if it were not an anxious, risky exploration of painful scenarios and a timid search for ways out of them. But those who consider themselves "practical" people don't perceive the irony—and are mystified when they keep getting sliced by their own pocketknives.)

6.213   This integration does violence to the essence of language.

6.2131   A violence that is just as necessary to "what language is," just as much part of its essence.

6.214   A definition of language based on its character as integrated
         is the (equally necessary) culmination of this act of violence.

6.2141   Such a definition reinforces the stunting of language's antici-
         pating character.

6.21411 A stunting that we call repression. Though no one is inten-
         tionally repressing anything. It (Es) just takes place. In the in-
         terest of the "ones," but not necessarily in ways that are "ac-
         cessible" to them, controlled by their "conscious planning."

6.21412 Conspiracy theories are not just stupid; they are also decep-
         tive and dangerous (again, not because someone is trying to
         deceive you!—the same problem keeps popping up at all lev-
         els). For it's often easy to prove that there is no conspiracy,
         and it's common to deduce from that trivial proof that there
         is nothing to worry about. (No intention "behind" it = no
         substance; or, how a bankrupt metaphysical scheme will help
         you not to see the abyss you are sinking in. Which may be
         exactly what you need to slow down the sinking process: if
         you got excited about it, you might cause a sudden collapse.
         But the eventual collapse may thus be more devastating.)

6.2142   Here we use "language" "ambiguously"—that is, we use it
         often (in line with "common sense") to refer to what is im-
         plied by this violating definition. We have to live through it;
         we cannot cancel it (without preserving it). We have to be-
         come stronger for it. The way to deal with a virus is by inocu-
         lating it—which is the basis of the dialectic. Mithridates al-
         ready knew all about it. And, when it surfaced again, it was
         with Jenner first and then with Hegel.

6.215   Part of what the violence amounts to consists of colonizing
         reference.

6.2151   Reference is no longer the adventurous connection with some-
         thing that might not (and might never) exist. It is rather
         the immediate, automatic association between two existing
         things.

6.21511 And, indeed, there is a problem now when reference is to
         what does not exist. What was the paradigm case, the whole
         point of the operation, has now become an embarrassing

anomaly, to be dispensed with, denied, rejected. That's really not a case of reference at all, you will say: it's a delusion to be dispelled, a "grammatical appearance" misrepresenting "true logical form." Or: you will turn it into a case of reference by making up an existing object that can function as what is being referred to (and never mind if that's *not* what one was talking about—if you have thus succeeded in cleverly changing the subject).

6.21512   Free logic is a symptom caused by this repression. So you will repress *it,* too (you will *cure* it). It's really nothing new, you will say, since I can translate it into restricted classical logic (and silence what is *lost* in that translation). Or I can make every sentence containing a reference to a nonexistent *false* (how convenient to have that kind of power! and how curious!). Or I can expand the universe of objects (bring in an "outer domain") and remain faithful to my repressive framework. That is, I can avoid hearing what the symptom is whispering. (Though it, irritatingly, continues to whisper, for example, reminding me of the annoying presence of singular terms that are not just nondenoting: they cannot possibly denote. But now at least I can think of that as a small, marginal problem—since a small, marginal place is all I have left for it. I can see myself irresistibly marching toward a complete solution. And what if that solution requires sacrificing round squares and assorted freaks? How much of a loss is that going to be?)

6.2152   The end of magical "evocation" and the beginning of "realism."

6.21521   Another bit of scum. "In the real world" things are such and such—an ignoble cover for the most outrageous schemes.

6.21522   Realpolitik—or, you will do whatever you can get away with, and then feel justified because you got away with it (and made it real in the process).

6.2153   The association between language and existing things was there from the beginning, but only as instrumental to a dialogue with what does not exist. Originally, I would use the association between, say, "chair" and chairs to speculate about "crazy" sorts of chairs, or "ideal" ones. To estrange myself from those specific bits of furniture with which I was stuck by concentrating on some "aspects" of them that I found to be "essential." (And thus, eventually, to *make* different chairs—to become "really" unstuck from the existing furniture.) Now, on the other hand, the nonexistent has faded away, and language has become enslaved to the real. Nuclear energy is at your service in the kitchen, running smoother, more powerful appliances. (The issue is, as always: what serves what else?)

6.22   In a language become public, *communication* occurs.

6.221   That is, the establishment of entrenched patterns where a specific linguistic performance by an agent is followed by a specific performance (linguistic or otherwise) by another agent.

6.2211   Once more, and in a self-conscious, self-satisfied manner: language as shorthand, as an economic tool for navigating the real. Bakers and bankers use "language," too. They use it "in order to" make bread and money. That is, in the course of doing so. Of getting fatter and richer. *Or* skinnier and poorer. And of proving their usage right by the weight of their bodies or vaults.

6.2212   The weight of the real. The anorexic rebellion of the unreal. The delicate balance between the two which is the weight of each of us. Which is my weight, too, the weight *I* have—the limit of the power "I" have on myself.

6.2213   The ultimate cunning: losing weight in order to be healthier. Protecting the existent from the overextension that might give the nonexistent a chance. Lean *and mean*. That is, professionally concerned with one thing only: survival itself. "Keep the sales tax in town. Shop Newport Beach."

6.2214   I would like to think that I am different. But shopping in town is—however minimally—a form of discipline. And I have been advocating discipline; I have been promoting humanism—that is, shopping within the human race. So it's not like I'm *not* mean, not guilty. It's rather that the choice is between guilt and suicide (or between two kinds of guilt: parochialism and universal destructiveness), and I choose the former. Which is a first, elementary, "automatic" form of courage. Then comes the more difficult, more important form: having the courage of one's courage. The guts to admit that it is indeed guilt you are accepting and living with. And that there must be something (some agony) to that—it can't be just words.

6.22141   The most difficult time comes immediately after your bravest move. You relax for a second, say something unimportant, *and that amounts to taking back your move.* For example: you make a forceful choice and then, pleased as you are with yourself, throw in a couple of rationalizing words. At which point you might as well forget it.

6.222   *This* language is no longer saying anything. It has become dumb—a necessary conceptual premise to (logically) posterior "empirical" developments (computers, etc.).

6.2221   Just as language is not necessarily verbal, not every verbal configuration is language. And this has little to do with the ideology superimposed on that configuration. There are lots of people speaking "in the name" of play, of nonbeing, of subversion; but the reference relation they work with is often one connecting solidly entrenched terms on both sides—their play and nonbeing and subversion are repetitive, calcified rituals that have lost (or never had) any capacity of anticipation (hence have nothing to do with *play* and *nonbeing* and *subversion*). These people, too, are saying nothing, just like the "utilitarians" they are so critical of (and however verbose the expectorations of both).

6.223   Something analogous to communication (which might still be called communication) occurs often wholly independently of language. And it is idiotically (but inevitably, and hence, in the end, "justly") assimilated with it. Body language and other similar aberrations. (Such aberrations have nothing to do with the fact that a language as we understand it may consist of bodily movements. For then there must be a story [not necessarily verbal] about the saving character of that dance. Once again, our enemy is not a specific language but a specific conception of what a language is.)

6.2231   Some will even consider this kind of talk evidence of the in-
          creasing importance of language. Adding insult to injury. De-
          priving language of its dignity after depriving it of its func-
          tion. And using language to do that dirty work. ("I" sure
          hope a day of reckoning will come for you!)

6.2232   The "linguistic turn" of Anglo-American analytic philoso-
          phy; or, the subjugating and torturing of a most powerful
          means of liberation presented as increased attention and re-
          spect for it. When you have power, you can really do and say
          whatever you want: even talk about "freedom fighters" and
          make it stick. (Not that it matters, really: blowtorching and
          decapitating opponents will take care of them anyway. But at
          least somebody—not the right people, for sure, not those who
          run things—would be ashamed. And who knows? There
          might even be practical consequences of that shame. Or so
          one would like to think. So you are afraid to think, which
          makes you want to have a backup option.)

6.224   Communication and (original) reference are orthogonal.

6.2241   An infant may have no language available (no capacity to ef-
          ficiently anticipate the future) and still utter sounds, and have
          those sounds influence other people's behavior in a regular
          way—which is all it takes for communication to be occurring.
          (I am not saying that this is so, if indeed it is—and I don't care
          about *that*—because the infant is not human, but only be-
          cause it does not have a complex and resilient enough struc-
          ture. Dolphins and geese may well do better in that respect.
          Which is why someone else—even, possibly, some later stage
          of "this" individual—might want to call *them* human.)

6.2242   That may be how language in fact gets started, but such is not
          our concern here. We are not doing (official) history: what we
          do precedes (and defies) the selection determining (that) his-
          tory. It does not deal with what (officially) happened, but with
          what *must,* or *can,* happen. Its point is to be beautiful—so as
          to gain strength (by better managing the strength it has). And
          maybe change the way history is written. Maybe hurt, too.

6.22421   There is nothing innocent about beauty. Its attractiveness
          simply *is* the power exercised on you by a pattern (sometimes

a foreign one, sometimes one of your own). For a moment (or for a while), that pattern will "look" to you like the attainment of the (deceptive) rational ideal of systematicity, it will look as if it had a satisfying response for any question you might ever have. But then you will switch to seeing the rabbit as a duck, and continue to pursue your true rational destiny by destroying that beautiful appearance. Unless its pattern has already destroyed *you*.

6.2243   Would it be possible to evolve from the automatic concatenation of moves we imagined in the infant's case to a similarly automatic behavior in the case of an adult? Can a human being go through his whole life without ever developing a language in our sense? Yes: that would be the denouement of some of the stories we would like to tell about contemporary society and technology. (And in order to tell those stories, we must be able to use the word "human" our way.)

6.225   Though they may, and often do, intersect.

6.2251   I may get you to bring me a slab by uttering, "Bring me a slab," and in this utterance "slab" may have (original) reference. There may be a longing voiced there that your performance will not appease, and this repeated failure will never stop puzzling us.

6.22511   "Tell me what it is that you need, so I can give it to you and once and for all you can stop bitching!" ("*Che vuoi?*")

6.2252   What "slab" refers to for me, the speaker, is a certain equivalence class. If you, the hearer, were to make the same utterance, "slab" would in general refer for you to a different equivalence class. But communication will still occur if in general you bring me what I expected you to bring me. (And remember: you and I may be housed in the same body. Nothing substantial is added by "outside" outsideness. Except more clarity. Or more confusion? The confusion of too much clarity—when you don't see that you have a problem, when you manage to avoid seeing that you have a problem by being perfectly transparent about it all?)

6.22521   (I have seen "philosophers" divide up a problem until it literally disappeared. By the end, I knew the problem was still there—it had to be, no one had addressed it—but I could no longer see where it was. The same kind of sophistry is often displayed by priests, or lawyers, or politicians: they confront an angry person, and show him that he can't really be angry *at* this or that or the other. By the end, the person is still angry, but no longer knows why [hence whether] he should be. Those "philosophers" ought to reflect on the analogy, on what it tells them about themselves and their practice—though, if they did, some of them would even take the analogy as a compliment.)

6.2253   Reference is to a speaker's "own objects," to members of his "own space" (once more: a speaker is not to be identified with a human body—there may be several speakers "lodged in" any such body). When successful communication occurs, there is a tendency to identify the relevant members of the relevant spaces (better: a tendency to *conceive* of this identity as possible or actual, and behave accordingly—"to identify" suggests illegitimately that both sides are equally available to someone performing an operation on them).

6.2254   Then one can also map the other person's linguistic performance within one's own space, and *via* this mapping *explain* that performance—which is what finding the *meaning* of the performance amounts to.

6.2255   The right metaphor of meaning is not, "By uttering X I *give* you something." It is rather, "You can tell yourself a story that makes my utterance unsurprising." That makes you feel the necessity of it. That makes it fall into place.

6.2256   A soothing operation. But, like everything else here, one that might strangle you.

6.22561 You start out trying to "interpret" what the guy said, to make his very words sound as the most rational occurrence, and find yourself generating more and more words, ever more different words, and invoking phantasms of your own, phantasms you would never have admitted as your own—but now you can, because they are "really" someone else's, so you can voice them, and listen to them at length. And one day they will claim your soul.

6.3   Even while conquered, language remains duplicitous.

6.31   It is still possible to use it to refer to what does not exist.

6.311   And this reference to the nonexistent infects "ordinary" talk. Ordinary declarative statements do nothing but express wishes. You say, "S is p," but all you *can* say, all you have grounds for, hence all you *mean* (all anyone else can say to make sense of your utterance), is, "I wish S were p." Dreams provide the paradigm for "reality": they show in a perfectly lucid manner the most diverse patterns coming on the scene and taking space and branching out—which is what "wishing" amounts to. And what fools you in dreams continues to fool you in reality—more so because there is much more of it, because in this context you have gotten (were forced to get) much better at it. Secondary elaboration, that is: the fitting of your various obscene, power-crazy, contradictory demands into a coherent, "nice" story.

6.3111   Aren't stories (among) the heroes of *this* story? So what's wrong with the comfort provided by secondary elaboration? What's wrong is that it comes with a story in the singular, and that may be comforting us to death: it may be the comfort to end all comfort. In order to handle (future) pain, we need stories, many of them. We need options and dialogue. (A single story is not even a story anymore. It has become the *truth*.)

6.312   It helps when things are less coherent, when we can see the mechanism of delusion fall apart, and the ugly creatures of darkness reveal their true colors. Think of the nastiness of an envious colleague's review of your work, or, on the other hand, of the sympathy and intelligence of your own reading of it. Communicative action, indeed! A solid basis for a disinterested inquiry!

6.313   That's how "deductive logic" can have currency. You would think that it's trivial to the point of silliness to take the trouble of constructing elaborate "arguments" to "prove" a conclusion that is at best as strong as your premises (and usually not as strong). But people enjoy contemplating their desires; and also, repetition makes them more real—we *want* to utter them loud and often, to the point when we begin to hear an echo. Something does happen as we move from premises to conclusion (or, here, from numbered paragraph to numbered paragraph): wish fulfillment is at work. We are lining up our regiments and getting them ready for war. And the more we look at them, the more we admire their uniforms and their orderly, colorful parade, the more confident we get about the truth of our position. ("How many divisions does the pope have?")

6.3131   But, though that is the intent, it might not be the outcome. Trying to impress people into military service often proves them more recalcitrant than one ever imagined. Watching their displays and war games often reveals weaknesses and inadequacies no one ever suspected. Similarly, logic's defensive moves might well have the effect of blowing up our cover (the one we were so sure about while it wasn't brought out in the open, while we were *only* sure about it).

6.314   As wishes are *realized* this way, voicing them is gradually transformed into providing a truthful account of reality. Expressions of wishes become the descriptive, declarative statements they are (often) supposed to be to the extent that on them no pressure is exercised, no criticism raised. So an effective way of generating descriptive accounts is by gathering people who agree on most basic matters (that is, on what they most basically want) and delegitimizing (or otherwise making irrelevant) any substantially different views (that is, wishes). Then indeed things "show up," can be "pointed out" and "recognized" (you may have never noticed that "I am sorry" is sort of intermediate between apologizing and conveying one's feelings, but as soon as I bring it to your attention it will strike you as a correct remark; after all, our feelings and our apologetic rituals—the ways we choose to think of ourselves feeling and apologizing—are so much alike). And if an outsider were to suggest an alternative, he would become the object of an inordinate (irrational? maybe, but remember that "rationality" is at stake here, that Machiavelli will be regarded by many as the epitome of the rational) amount of aggressiveness, and the target of all sorts of vicious ad hominem attacks. (Ironically, he will often be accused of "wishful thinking.") Suddenly anything is possible, and no move is shameful: it's like a rat finding itself in the wrong pack and not smelling right—and being cut to pieces without mercy. So that cosmos can be restored.

6.3141 Later reality will be defined in terms of these "realistic" accounts. The world will become the (intentional) object of a "theory" (here I am using the word in the derogatory sense in which people say "Evolution is only a theory"). Where the danger (from a purely parochial point of view—leaving absolute freedom aside) is one of forgetting the role of disagreement and deviance, of being too reassured about (again) a single system of wishes. It is just when it is too powerful—to the point of having no credible enemies—that an empire begins to collapse, to rot, to degenerate from within. One wonders why.

6.3142 To reiterate: the problem is not that wishes are expressed under the guise of "constative" speech acts but that only some are. And the primordial significance of those acts comes across most openly when declarative statements are simply, starkly opposed to one another. "It's my word against yours." (Which, of course, may be a ruse, and a cheap one, but doesn't have to be, and often is not. Often both interlocutors are indeed in the grips of their tenacious desires.)

6.3143 "Empirical studies conducted in the last fifteen years show that depressed people tend to have a more accurate perception of reality." How sad! But shouldn't that tell you something about your notions of reality and accuracy? Isn't it the case that you are identifying "an accurate perception of reality" with the state someone is in when he no longer cares about *doing* anything? When he no longer has any *real* wishes? When he has totally succumbed to a single overpowering pattern? And isn't your sad "appreciation" of the situation another example of the same attitude?

6.31431 Incidentally, you should reflect on your talk of "rational choice." For people accurate in your sense would hardly ever *make* any choice; hence that talk would end up having virtually no application. People would end up being either inactive or irrational. Do you suppose there could be a political significance to this conclusion? (Or is it just, again, an "accurate" one?)

6.31432   Of course, what *you* mean by "rational choice" does not have the dignity of a *choice* (or of something *rational*). You think that people are *given* a certain preference profile (as *what they are*), and then all they have to "do" is perform a few silly, cute computations. So what *you* have "done" is appropriate these words to your depressing view of humanity.

6.32   In sum, it is still possible for language to resist its integration into entrenched patterns.

6.33   Though in general reductive of pain in the long run, this resistance is painful at the time.

6.331   At least insofar as it resists entrenchment.

6.34   Force will be exercised to overcome this resistance, and avoid current pain.

6.341   Once again, to avoid the unreal.

6.35   This force will manifest itself by inhibiting any use of language outside entrenched patterns.

6.351   Language will be forced into the procrustean bed of language *games*.

6.3511   Games one is supposed to win? What is at stake? Who referees? Reality, you say? No kidding.

6.3512   "Reality" is what this whole conception is supposed to shore up. What would be hard put to be (real), except for the efficacy of this conception. It is anything but a neutral judge.

6.3513   I have seen judges like that. Maybe I have *only* seen judges like that.

6.3514   I have heard people say that if all judges are like that, then there can be nothing wrong with it. (People who obviously don't know—or don't want to know, would rather forget— what "wrong" is.)

6.352   *Rules* will be imposed on it. With exceptions, of course, needed as usual to prove the rule. Multiplicity will have to be exceptional—there will have to be something extraordinary about it.

6.3521 One will make a big deal of linguistic connections being "arbitrary." Not reflecting on the other major resonance of that word: "despotic," "tyrannical." Not grasping its subterranean message.

6.3522 A classic case of regimentation: the illocutionary "force" of certain expressions. Which amounts to their no longer having any force, to their being *forced* into a single reading. A necessary premise for language finally "doing things" (or, more honestly, for things being done *to* language).

6.35221 The paradigm of illocutionary force: "I am carrying a bomb," uttered at the security checkpoint of an airport. *This utterance will not be taken as a joke:* if you say, "I am carrying a bomb," you will be carrying it—that is, you will be treated as one who does. You will have successfully baptized yourself a bomb carrier.

6.35222 None of that "intention" business that confused Austin and led Searle completely astray. If you say, "I promise," while intending to deceive, you can still be held to it. And sometimes you use that to your advantage. You say, "But I did apologize," as if that were enough. As if it weren't clear to all involved that you didn't mean it. (That the most conspicuous associations mobilized by your statement do not provide a credible explanation of your whole performance.) And still no one could "legitimately" blame you for being such a cheat. "Conventions" come to "your" help.

6.35223 The uniqueness of this interpretation will stick as long as the social structure maintaining it is cohesive enough. Which will be the case more in more "serious" (e.g., more dangerous) circumstances (as in the military, where logic belongs). But irony will always threaten this cohesiveness, and so will play, and irritation, and hypocrisy. And crime.

6.35224 And love. Could you really make promises to a lover? A child, a parent? Could they really make you fulfill them—without ceasing to be lovers, or parents, or children? Could you apologize to them? Tell them "I am carrying a bomb" in such a way

that you would *then* be carrying it? (Or, "I'm carrying your
child.")

6.35225   In fact, all of the above is becoming less absurd, more credible
as we speak. The so-called fragmentation of the social structure is a con issue, an insolent travesty of a problem. What is
happening is rather that the social structure is becoming more
powerful; its rules are insinuating themselves into the most
"private" contexts. Including linguistic rules—the rack on
which language is chained. In the resulting system of total administration, your lovers and children and parents will take
you to court, demanding payment for the promissory notes
you (inadvertently?) talked yourself into. (You should never
speak with your pants down—just take care of business. And
hope that body "language" doesn't come back to haunt you.)

6.3523   But multiplicity will get its revenge: you will not be able to
establish any rule—for any sequence. The hallucinatory character of your pronouncements will become clear, for those
who have eyes to see. Others, of course, will be more than
happy to "think" that they are not (yet?) being smart enough,
and will joyfully continue to look. After all, that's what
"happy" means: thoughtless.

6.353   Academies will be constituted to codify language's *proper* use.
And they will occasionally display benevolent, destructive tol-
erance toward "difference." Making sure that they label it;
once you know that something is "slang," you are no longer
to worry about it. It no longer concerns you.

6.3531   But it's amazing how strict these asylums get when it comes
to administering their rites of passage. Try to use slang in a
dissertation! (It's quite another story when you are already
a member of the clan. Then everyone knows it's tongue in
cheek; everyone knows you are only "quoting" it.)

6.35311   (A quote: a cowardly tactic to speak your desire without admitting to it. Worse: while blaming it on someone else. The
paradigmatic case of quote: those moralistic—or scholarly—
frauds who get to talk nonstop about pornographic material
without being infected by it. Except that of course they are.)

6.35312   (Sometimes quoting your desire is the best you can do, in preparation for better times to come. Wonder why there are so many quotes here?)

6.354   Schooling will enforce the transmission of entrenched patterns from one generation to the next. (Notice my resistance to calling this activity "education." Not that it "isn't" education, of course, or that the resistance will succeed. But it still matters: we can't always take an understanding, world-historical view of things. Sometimes we are hurt, and it shows, and it ought to show.)

6.3541   Kids are *told* the right use of a word. That is, they are told *what to do*. What an interesting contrast with being *told* a story at bedtime! What a bloody battle is being fought on that little word! Over those little people!

6.3542   What good is Latin to me? There is a point to this question. As long as it does not mean: How much richer am I going to get by learning (some meager rudiments of) Latin? As long as it means: What good is it to me to practice a language *as* dead, as a tired routine? As *essentially* past?

6.35421   The triumph of repression: having a whole dead language "on line." Conquered once and for all—indeed, conquered twice, by death and by this postmortem. Permanently dissected and organized. If only all languages could be treated that way, like certain dissected, organized neighborhoods! Wouldn't it be nice, and safe? (A good, persuasive way of getting the point across is: Think about your children venturing outside absurdly protective suburbs, about their helplessness. About how the security of a situation perfectly under control—and the consequent lack of familiarity with any kind of "experimental" behavior, with any *life*—is responsible for that helplessness. Start sweating.)

6.35422   Though, if "one" feels too safe about it, it is precisely within this cemetery that new life can grow. Corpses fester; worms prosper in them. "They are the ultimate conquerors."

6.355   People will be stigmatized as of lower (public) value when they use language inappropriately.

6.3551   The same thing is happening now with "computer literacy."

Of course computers open up a new area of "play," but most people don't really *play* in it. What emerges instead (right away, before the new technology has a chance to create havoc) is the establishment of a new "grammar" and new "dutiful" tasks. You *must* be up on them if you want to be part of the (proper) crowd. You *must* be able to access the library of Alexandria, though you will not read anything in it. You would feel that you were missing out on something important, on something *yours*, if you did not have available things you will never use—because your time is spent satisfying the need to acquire them. Once more, the territory of freedom has been occupied by necessity.

6.3552   But this "tool" will play (with) *you*. *And* win. Primarily because you will not know that there was play going on, or *what* sort of play it was.

6.36   The multiplicity of (linguistic) patterns will be the most effective vehicle of continued resistance.

6.361   An alternative pattern might occur infrequently (we then call it *dormant*).

6.362   But it might also itself become entrenched (though perhaps to a lesser degree than the most entrenched).

6.363   In general, this alternative pattern will be denied referential value.

6.3631   Because reference has been publicly appropriated.

6.364   So its referential character will be understood in terms of *association*, of *resonance*, of *rhetoric*.

6.3641   The physical traits of language will be called in question—the physical thickness of words.

6.3642   A paradox, because these physical traits will be regarded as the residue of the languagehood of language, as a manifestation of its impurity, whereas language here is precisely doing its thing: resisting "normalization" by playing one entrenchment against another. (Just as people were once able to play one evil empire against the other. Now they no longer have such luck.)

6.36421   One of the many paradoxes caused by the enforcement of power. Power distorts the geometry of our social space. It makes people cross-eyed. Blinders will do that sort of thing to you.

6.365   So rhetoric is subversive.

6.3651   Without specifying subversive of what.

6.3652   The general point is: it inclines one to go beyond repetitive behavior.

6.36521   Action is subversive. Action is subversion. Action is when you *do* something, and nothing is done when you mechanically respond to expectations. Dead calm again: the jogging in place that most of our "action" reduces to.

6.3653   *How* does language do that? Uttering sounds (or inscribing characters) is one of many things that can be done, one of many (human) practices. So how is it possible that this practice have a stimulating effect on the others, that words make people do things?

6.36531   No such problem exists for traditional theories—at the cost of underwriting the silliness of the practical syllogism. You *want* something, *know* how to get it, and proceed to *act* accordingly. Through language, you disseminate your knowledge, so as to make others able to perform the same routine. But, of course, this scheme is constantly contradicted by the way people "work." No one is ever moved to action by knowledge, even when a strong desire is present. No one is ever cured of a neurosis by being told about its causes (and believing them).

6.36532   It's not just that there are "exceptions" to the practical syllogism (that occasionally people are "incontinent"—or are they, *really?*); there is no case in which this is a reasonable account of what is going on, in which awareness of means and ends determines our behavior. The reverse is often the case: our behavior often echoes in the corridors of consciousness. In this sense, we don't do what we say, we rather say what we do; so, clearly, it is not in this sense that language can bring about action.

6.36533 But the relation between words and things does not end there. We know that language provides a relatively safe lab where to try substitutes of action without paying (all) the price of the real thing, and that occasionally these substitutes spread into "real" action. The problem is how the spreading works, what makes the difference between the things I think of doing *but don't do* and the ones I think of doing *and do*—and maybe even make *others* do (who did not spend much time thinking about them). And it's an enormous problem: it amounts to how nonbeing can push being into nonbeing, and itself become being, despite all the defense mechanisms being has in place. We can imagine that in moments of serious crisis, when those mechanisms are overburdened, anything might happen, and even tenuous patterns might come to the fore. But such moments are rare, and words can cause people to do things even in perfectly ordinary (noncritical) circumstances.

6.36534 To explain this possibility we must go back to sounds, to the *music* of language. We can be affected by sounds without paying attention to them, we noted earlier; now we must focus on what exactly affects us—on what the music *is*. The music of language is its physical thickness: the multiplicity of overlapping patterns that are "left over" after we account for the "official" one(s) in which language is entrenched. Several of these other patterns are themselves entrenched, usually by being integrated in larger patterns that have nothing "linguistic" about them: *natural* patterns that already have a hold on us, to which we are already committed—the rhythm of our walking, say, or our eating, our lovemaking, our fighting. So, as we are spoken to (possibly by ourselves), these other patterns can grab us, and as we are grabbed by them, our moves will tend to fall into *the same* patterns. Which will bring into relief one of the many different things we could be doing (maybe one that otherwise would have been very unconspicuous), and make it the one we *are* doing. The unnatural becoming of action is thus kept on course by being assimilated to natural becoming; its absurdity is facilitated and stabilized as if by a gigantic flywheel. (You act by making yourself into a nonagent, by letting something bigger than you flow through your body. Then you will probably wake up, and "re-

alize" what you did. Action is always in retrospect.) That's
what rhyme does to you, or a song's chorus. That's the origin
of the very first chants (true blueprints for action, and em-
phatically not for what they *say*): sexual chants, war chants,
labor chants. (Mimicry again—think of Plato's *Republic,* or
Aristotle's *Politics.*) You commit people to certain words, to
what they "mean"—to their associations, to the promises
(the wishes) they express—before they even listen to them (we
can go years without understanding the lyrics of songs we
like, and we still "sing" them). Because you make them *do*
what those promises involve before they know *that* they are
doing it. Later, when they find out, they will also find themselves in possession of words they are now "hearing" for the
first time, and will use them to rationalize what they did. And
one can only hope it's not a lynch mob that this "inspiring"
rhetoric is letting loose.

6.36535   An uneasy coexistence, in language, of "content" and music.
Where the latter is quickly dismissed as irrelevant, while it's
doing all the work—better still, *so that* it can (quietly) do all
the work (funny that music, of all things, should work quietly, without being heard)—of turning other people's wheels
(or indeed your own: you need to jump-start yourself, occasionally, to give yourself a little motivational speech—which
will only work if it *sounds* right). But those who are in the
motivational business (advertisers, politicians, military com-
manders) know all about jingles, hymns, and marching songs.
They know that a message must "ally" itself with music if it is
to be heeded, that the music must *distract* the audience from
the message, attract the audience to *its own* pattern while it
carries the message across. They know that any reference to
people's "interests" is an evasion—however well intentioned,
however "progressive" it might be. Any person is a manifold
of disparate, conflicting interests; therefore, saying that the
lynch mob is "protecting its position of domination and privilege" amounts to refusing to look into the details of the operation, into how a certain music will make a certain pattern
emerge—a certain position, a certain system of goals, *as opposed to any other options that were equally available.* And
how consequently the music will make people perform certain

actions, whereas a different tune would have made the same people act differently.

6.36536   The very first thing music will make you do is dance. So that's the paradigm of how to do things with words. Before I perform any action, I will execute "the same moves" as steps in a dance. Before anything shows up as work, it existed as play. And there is always music in the background of play; music is always being played.

6.36537   This music and dance will then be remembered, that is, reenacted with relentless periodicity, as the (life) rhythms they are. Though, in order for specific contents to be remembered, we generally need more expressive means, such as are provided by specific musical phrases: individual memories are generally associated with individual melodies. Without a melody, all you usually remember—that is, (watch yourself) reenact—is that *something* was going on, and possibly excited you a great deal. With a melody, on the other hand, a definite experience will come (back) to mind, whether or not you want it. Jingles you hate—and hate yourself for being obsessed by—will continue to surface, *and will guide you through the aisles of the supermarket.* Marching songs will continue to make your hair rise, however horrible or ridiculous their lyrics. You will try to protect yourself from such irritatingly easy *Blitzkriege,* such overwhelmingly powerful weapons: send signals of anxiety (of disgust, of contemptuousness) whenever a tune is too "catchy." You will look for atonality, for noise—and in the process might make yourself even more vulnerable: when the rhythm has prepared you for unspecified action, any minimal spark can set you off, even in directions you ordinarily (when "under control") would have vehemently resisted.

6.3654   But doing something is bad. It hurts. It does not leave well enough alone. It is *evil.*

6.36541   Action is evil. That is what "being responsible" for one's actions ultimately refers to. That is what you find yourself staring at as soon as the music stops—and you begin to count the corpses. (Apocalypse, now: a *now* that suddenly imposes itself with terrifying, nauseating vividness.)

6.36542   Every action is revolutionary, if only in a small scale. It's the
          arrogant affirmation of *one* project against many others, the
          overweening imposition of a specific presence. There will be
          heads rolling as a result, and blood spilled, and somebody will
          cry foul. And a moral (that is, a resentful) judgment will be
          made.

6.3655   So action must be guarded against. *Counter*acted, possibly
          annihilated. Except that those who have more power will be
          more successful in doing this, and preserving their structure.
          They will utilize a moral vocabulary as they do so, of course,
          since that vocabulary is integrally related to the whole opera-
          tion; but the reason why *their* moral judgments (their resent-
          ment, their envy) get more currency is just that they (can)
          speak louder.

6.37   The public that has appropriated language will attempt to
          neutralize its resistance.

6.371   First and foremost, by making itself felt, by being present and
          calling attention to the (attempted) subversion. The enemy
          will not be able to operate in the dark; there will be (envious,
          unfriendly) *eyes* directed at him. Watching his every step, ex-
          posing it, making a spectacle of it.

6.372   And, concurrently, blaming it, stigmatizing it, loading it with
          guilt.

6.373   One thus acquires a conscience, *that is,* a consciousness (*co-
          scienza*): a suspicious, unsympathetic gaze contemplating *and
          disapproving of* all my "inner" workings. Disapproving in
          principle, *whatever* those workings might be. It's not like you
          could be innocent in the face of consciousness (that's what we
          will call it, though we just said it is also conscience, since we
          don't want to be locked in a "moral" ghetto: we want moral-
          ity to spread, we want to bring out the political implications
          of any "purely" phenomenological analysis — "to the things
          themselves" and all such crap).

6.3731   This is, finally, Consciousness capitalized: the thing, or place,
          where a search for my "self" is ordinarily supposed to begin.
          From now on, I will not capitalize it; so, to avoid confusion,
          I must specify how this "consciousness" differs from (and re-

lates to) what we have already encountered under that name. So far, consciousness was the ironical position from which some element of my multiplicity can view some other such element. A great resource, we know already: as I unconsciously wander around a familiar environment (and, most often, am just as unconsciously immersed in some pleasant fantasy), something can go wrong, in which case it is useful to "wake up" and take a critical, unsympathetic look at what is happening. A parent's look, say, or a driving instructor's, or a policeman's. But that "consciousness" has no "stream," no continuity: as soon as the problem is solved, I go back to sleep. And it's not consistent, *it had better not be:* the more irregular or dissonant my skipping from one perspective to another is, the more it can help. Whereas the new character surfacing now is supposed to be constantly living one single coherent life. (It isn't, of course; but the ideology is so powerful that it gets people to nod.)

6.37311   As always, this new character comes into being by adapting structures already in place. But here the adaptation issues in a radical reversal. It's one thing when fins turn into wings, and it's quite another when the general ability to assume different points of view is put at the service of repressing difference.

6.3732   Consciousness is not me, indeed is not even *mine*. It is essentially other. It is inimical and destructive of me, of mineness.

6.37321   Not insofar as it is one more voice speaking "inside"—one more element of that outsideness which "inside" is, which has largely been confined inside—but insofar as it intends to cancel all other voices, except to the extent that it can rule over them, have them agree with itself.

6.37322   The paradox of liberalism: you cannot be liberal with those who would cancel liberalism itself. (The liar all over again: making room for the liar belongs to the destiny of any rich, articulate structure. *Which is a feature and not a mistake.* You don't want to fix it; you want to learn to live with it. To become acquainted with the complex negotiations that are required by this sort of structure—and would not be required by a simpler one, whence the recurring temptation to simplify matters, to read the feature as a mistake.)

6.37323 Though you might still want to hear them. It might help you a lot (help the plurality "you" are) to know their tactics. To have them, too, speak "within" yourself. Immunization, once more. I want to hear what Hitler has to say, hear it to the end, in all of its twists and turns; having him shut up "inside" could give more power to the real Hitlers, give more of a surprise element to their attacks. (Defensiveness is a poor defense strategy, and squeamishness a poor way of handling fear. Just as feeling paralyzed does not help when you are fleeing from an aggression—indeed, it does help *the aggressor,* and you should reflect on what that tells you about "yourself.")

6.37324 Don't make too much of those Nazi speeches being stupid. Don't feel too superior, for *that* would be stupid (or worse). Remember: it's the music that matters. Even when it is a monotone, for that too resonates with (is built upon) a life rhythm (indeed, one of the most common and seductive), hence it too can get people to act (if the right signal is sent at the right time, when the monotone has completely enthralled them). And you need to see that; you don't want to be too smart for your own good.

6.3733 Consciousness is a control mechanism serving the public: defending it from the deviance that *I* represent.

6.37331 That is, from what in me is not just another object: another predictable structure. From the "I" that *I* (in part) am. (And hence also protecting what *else* I am from "myself." As when you get too close to a sharp knife, and could—and would like to—stick it into somebody's throat, and singing some silly, childish song is frighteningly not enough to stop you [to bring out the helpless child in you]: you may need to speak to yourself about it, even aloud. May need to get sick to your stomach by *consciously* facing that course of action, with as many of its consequences as you can manage to evoke.)

6.37332 From multiplicity, from ambiguity, from displacement. From the subject.

6.37333 No wonder the soul is considered immortal then. The public that has appropriated me will certainly survive, long after *my* game is over, and so will its image of how well or ill I behaved. (It will make me pay forever for those actions of mine it didn't like, or continue in perpetuity to pat me on the back. And it doesn't matter that I am no longer there, and no longer have a back: they must make an example of me.)

6.37334   No wonder there is not much consciousness during sleep (there is, indeed, only when the censor feels that things are getting out of hand—and is ready to sound the alarm clock). The physical paralysis that characterizes that situation is in general enough of a guarantee against the dangers of subjectivity.

6.3734   But it is forced upon me, and I am forced to identify with it, and eventually I do. I (am made to) become my consciousness. It becomes the most transparent form of access to my most intimate, most fundamental truth.

6.37341   A true case of identification with the aggressor. Which, as all other such cases, not so much protects me from being hurt as it makes me not acknowledge the pain I feel (as bit after bit of me gets destroyed). Or not do justice to it—treat it as the dignified, meritorious agony of climbing a steep hill. Except that here I am climbing out of myself, and "getting to the top" means being totally washed out. (It's like feeling good at the end of a "hard day" of the most senseless busywork, the most vicious, unjust "killing" of one's time. And this is more than an analogy: you are your time, so appropriating that time, making it subservient to an empty performance, empties your being, leaves it in total control of the public. Once the habit is built of this [dis]appropriation, the theory of it will come easy. Forcing you [or enticing you] to feel pain for a trifle is an obvious strategy for making you assign a high value to that trifle—and no value to what matters. At some level you sense the connection between value and pain [the pain of pushing your structure to the limit, the value of the diversity and flexibility thus acquired], so you might even be prodded by it to work at things of value, unless the pain is provided "for free," attached to "just anything." As strong emotions are in amusement parks—the thrill of jumping without really jumping, hence without learning to jump.)

6.37342 As most victims, I end up subscribing to the aggressor's agenda. Kissing its hands. (He must love me, since he's beating me so hard.)

6.37343 And judging consciousness to be a miraculous occurrence, something in which the whole universe finds its justification, which the whole world history was preparing—and certainly something that holds the key for making sense of that unique, amazing kind of occurrence which I am. (Here apes get forgotten again, however dutifully you kneeled before the lessons of "science.")

6.37344 *Arbeit macht frei.* The thousand-year Reich. Though that one only lasted twelve years, its propaganda was on the right track. The first thing you need to do if you want your bluff to stick is to rewrite history accordingly: as the laborious but irresistible vindication of the ideal.

6.37345 As was suggested earlier, the identification we are talking about is not with a real structure but with an ideology (once more, it expresses a wish). For the repressive consciousness is no more continuous than the ironical one: it too comes in fits and starts, whenever it's needed. The public would certainly be better served if I were caged in a (permanently guarded) panopticon, but that would be too much of a waste of precious resources; so the best it can do is to make me *believe* that there is always a guard watching me (*and that I am the guard*). The nice thing about it (for the public) is: that belief can never be proved wrong, since if I challenged it I would automatically make the guard show up. (Have you ever tried thinking of something no one ever thought of? And does that prove that *there are* no things no one ever thought of?)

6.37346 The next epicycle in this deluded game: *esse est percipi*, the comedy of empirical idealism. The whole world is what (and how it) appears to consciousness. Which makes one feel all-powerful, a true creator. Whereas it's the public that is doing it: after expropriating you, throwing you out of "your own" space, they are using you to legitimate universal expropriation. To seal the instrumental occupation of the world, its reduction to the ghostly counterpart of technological mastery.

(It's not by chance, then, that subjectivism and the industrial revolution surface together—the above is one of their many profound resonances.)

6.3735   Consciousness enforces consistency on the subject (again, only "theoretically," but often that is enough—its consequences are repressive enough). Most of what the subject is is sacrificed on its altar. And (conscious) memory is used to keep track of what has now truly become *one's* "subject."

6.37351 Wonder why you forget things you "should" remember? Things you *would* indeed remember if there were just one of you, as the ideology has it. But there isn't, so a lot of disturbance occurs, a lot of noise, and you need to shift back into the right character before the right things can come back to you. That is, before the will to power associated with (or constituting) the relevant pattern can play out its tendency to (eternally) recur.

6.37352 It gets worse as you advance in age, and you take that to be a sign of degeneration. You associate "old" with "weak" and you cook up (or buy ready-made) an ideal of youth as perfect health—which gives the whole game away. What happens instead is that growth as a human being amounts to extending the play and the number of characters that use one's body; so a young person is in general less human than an older one (though also, in general, more willing to *become* human— having fewer scars, having suffered less in this process, not quite knowing what it's all about). Youth's health and vigor are manifestations of a unilateral, scaled-down subjectivity; and the later weariness, incongruity, and (occasional or permanent) forgetfulness intimate that the body is doing what it ought to—stretching itself to the utmost, making room for a larger set of personalities. At some point, of course, it will break, but so what? If you don't like that, lock yourself in a vault and practice your beauty sleep! (Or, instead, get *extremely* tired and then see what happens: it is just when you are ready to burst at the seams that you are the closest to finding yourself.)

6.38   The notion of privacy continues to evolve.

6.381   "Earlier" (in our narrative) privacy was opposed to the public
        as transgression is to repetition (even if transgression is "ulti-
        mately" in the interest of repetition). As the unreal is to the
        real. As multiplicity is to uniformity.

6.3811 Each cluster of resistance was a "point of light" in the strug-
        gle against the public. That was a major implication of lan-
        guage being essentially private, since the relevant de*priva*tion
        was an effective tactic in this struggle. (You wouldn't want
        to deal with virus outbreaks or nuclear meltdowns when they
        spread out of control, but *if* you can control them effectively,
        and learn from them, such outbreaks and meltdowns are
        precisely what you are after, what you want to produce—
        Prometheus and all that. So the "if" clause brings out a liber-
        ating state of affairs: revolution in a bottle maybe, but still
        revolution—indeed, revolution *thanks to* the bottle, and espe-
        cially the cork.)

6.382   "Later," as privacy is less and less able to help the cause of
        freedom, it comes to be identified with each of the little cells
        in which transgression is locked, constantly afraid of the pub-
        lic eye, constantly in the wrong. Eventually, the focus shifts
        entirely away from the *content* of what is being "private"—
        that is, denied access, insulated, refused the possibility of act-
        ing out, *and also*, because of that, provided with some room,
        given a definite chance of development and growth—to dep-
        rivation per se, even if what happens within "privacy" is a
        tired replica of what happens "out there." People get all flus-
        tered about invasions of their privacy, and about defend-
        ing themselves from such invasions, though nothing there is
        worth invading or defending—though all there is to it is
        catechistic conformism. (But there is a point to having them
        strenuously attached to this empty package, of course: that
        way, they might not miss what they are really being deprived
        of, which is no longer just access. God—or the party, or Big
        Brother—has indeed entered their bedroom, and is regulating
        the proceedings there. And they no longer notice.)

6.3821 Liberating games—*different* liberating games—could be
        played with (and by) limited numbers of people when the

rules were written by those very people. When they decided, say, what to count as beautiful and exciting (irregular teeth, a mole—sometimes called a "beauty spot"). Now the rules are universal, we are supposed to wear our flesh and bone the way clothing was once worn (as a decoration under *every-one's* eyes), and the space of freedom has narrowed down to a vanishing point. All our most intimate (physical) re-cesses have been legislated into proper shape (that is, muscu-lar shape—there is no longer any softness, any uncertainty to it, it's all hard, all perfectly "defined") and enslaved to tedious routines. Which doesn't mean that everything about us is "up to par" (hardly!), but it does mean that we don't (want to) see ourselves in what isn't. A good way of defusing (or maybe in-stigating, as a powerful means of deception?) the "sexual lib-eration." After virtual fear, virtual love is next.

6.38211   How about "fat is beautiful" then? Are the people proclaim-ing such slogans opposed to the public invasion of one's space? No more than the losers in a corporate merger are op-posed to capitalism.

6.3822   We can still play games in our minds, still retreat to our "true" self behind the flesh and bone. Yeah, right. As if that were the easiest thing in the world. It's actually among the hardest, and the most unstable. (In part because the patterns of those games are denied any echoes, and consequently es-tablish little credibility even within ourselves, and fizzle out. We think of them as our little idiosyncratic elements of mad-ness—except for being surprised by the agreement we find when we decide to make an indecent exposure of them.)

6.3823   In practice, selves have been annihilated—reduced to *noth-ings*. And any nothing is like any other. So you can give them complete "freedom" to do what they want. No risk there: they will all want the same things, the things you told them to, those you have decided to drop into their empty wells.

6.3824   There was a time when we did notice this repressive move, and felt its "otherness." Then we thought that a universal eye was watching all of us simultaneously, that it was here, there, and everywhere. That there was no escaping it—nothing would block it out. It was a jealous, violent, rabid eye, one that would not be appeased. It knew all about us, and hated us. It caused fear and trembling.

6.38241 That, incidentally, is where the *esse est percipi* first found its (natural) place. The Bishop still needed the outside eye (precisely *as* outside, as a party to an outside/inside confrontation) to put together a world for him. He had not totally identified with the predator and was ready to tell God what *He* was supposed to do. When identification is complete, we won't worry about ensuring that the world be *true* to some standard; we will advance no demands on it. We will take what comes and be perfectly happy with it, perfectly reassured that everything is all right. Postmodern "fragmentation" will triumph, and utter market expropriation with it. Under the guise of rampant "difference," which will now be all over the place and matter not at all. Difference without agony, difference pure, difference that is not *from* something, *against* something, no longer makes a difference. We get an empty word after the "thing" has been stolen. (In a mall, the most disparate, different products are sold *next* to one another—no real competition there, no real choice; the ideology is that you can have everything, one day this, the next day that, in an indefinite progression, an indefinitely progressing pyramid scheme. You now *are* God; or rather, now God has gulped you down.)

6.38242 (Sometimes your visual field includes a choice of a large number of different "ethnic" restaurants, where you will be happy to occasionally "entertain" yourself and others. Thus confirming your established routines instead of challenging them, as tourism in general does—how nice to come back from all those strange, silly places and customs to the comfort of one's own home! You have seen it, appreciated it, and pushed it aside—pushed it into *asideness.*)

6.38243 Christianity is an interesting midway station in this development. As God becomes human, He also becomes more loving and generous. The terror associated with His omniscient, unrelenting eye is calmed down when He begins to look at us with a benevolent smile. Or at least that's the idea—though we continue to feel terrorized, and can't quite understand our reaction to such a friendly, genial parental figure. (Even less will we be able to understand it when God is no longer needed—not as someone else, that is—when we have entirely identified with the source of the terror. A terror we nonetheless, perplexingly, still continue to feel.)

6.3825   This is not all there is to religion; but it is all there is to "religion within the limits of reason alone." To religion within the limits of the "rational" (of that rational which "the real" was made to be, whatever the casualties).

6.383   Throughout this development, privacy is intimately related to silence. Not because there is something necessarily unspoken about (the content of) what is private (on the contrary, we know that that content often is a conversation—indeed, a constant, *loud* debate) but because the act of making it private consists of severing connecting lines, and ordinary, "empirical" silence (the sort of thing we unquestioningly call silence) is how this interruption, this cut, most obviously shows up (for those who are left out).

6.3831   You become silent before certain people (your parents, say). Not just because your mouth does not utter (certain) sounds: your whole body is silent about certain moves, acts, experiments, *desires* (one desires, and hence one speaks, with all of one's body, all of one's form of life). And that doesn't mean you are silent period, it doesn't mean *any* of your moves, acts, experiments, desires go absolutely unspoken. On the contrary, that's precisely when you need an intimate circle of coconspirators, an underground network where to try out all those different parts of yourself.

6.3832   Considerable skill is needed to keep subjectivity going in total silence. Not everyone can make the move from reading aloud to quietly moving one's lips (my father has always read that way), and eventually to doing it all "in one's head." It takes discipline, it takes exercise, *and* it takes going through the various stages in order, ontogenetically as well as phylogenetically. You can't start at the end and still read—or be a subject. (Just as you can't start doing additions on a calculator and learn anything but how to punch keys.) You will be staring at the page, but no music will play for you.

6.38321   And some of those for whom the music has played, and is per-
          haps still playing, will try to convince you that it's just as
          well—that "writing" is what is truly liberating, that you
          can (and should) forget the music. And, if you believe them,
          they will have castrated you—something they keep talking
          about, as if to make light of it, while they are in the process
          of doing it.

6.3833   Nor can anyone constantly sustain this development. Occa-
          sionally, there will be a need for shifting back. For reading
          aloud to increase concentration. Or for going into a sound-
          proof room and screaming your head off, to reassure yourself
          of the concrete, physical reality of your moves—however
          "private" they might (have turned out to) be. It will happen,
          most often, under pressure: when things crack, they show
          more of their texture.

6.38331   Nothing is less revealing than grace, or peace, or health: the
          point of all of them is to prevent you from noticing where
          they come from and what they are made of.

6.3834   At a certain stage in this development, it becomes politically
          expedient to erase its origin. Disconnecting the subject from
          its humus, from the ground where it still needs to return pe-
          riodically to regain strength, making it misunderstand the sig-
          nificance of those returns, of the need for them, having it read
          them as disturbances, as (mental) illness, is an effective way
          of really turning it into an invalid. (Keep Antaeus up in the
          air, and eventually you will be able to strangle him. Tell An-
          taeus his *home* is up in the air, make him believe it, and you
          won't even have to waste any of your energy.) More than a
          rewriting of history will occur: it will be a true canceling of
          it. History has never happened. Ideas have not painfully is-
          sued from delicate surgery, which somehow managed to keep
          them half alive while redirecting all blood circulation away
          from them. (Was it perhaps *cryo*surgery? Is a drastic lowering
          of the temperature essential to its "success"? Is reason neces-
          sarily cold?) Ideas have always been; better, they "are" tense-
          lessly. No reference to action, to anything that takes place in
          time, is relevant to their essence. They are to be contemplated.
          Vision is the proper way of relating to them, since (you feel—

but we know that that's wrong) it is the most detached of senses, the one that most relates to things *as they are.*

6.39   But consciousness can itself become a vehicle of transgression. Though without honor, it is still a prophet. Though for the "wrong" reasons, it still announces (the coming of difference).

6.391   Points of connection can be used by both parties, whichever party (with whatever intent) put them there in the first place.

6.3911   Like the police, prison guards, spies. Priests. All of them always already corrupted, smeared, contaminated by their middleness, their role as intermediaries. (You do need the concept of diplomatic immunity, just as you need many other such oxymorons. And, if you are strong enough, you may be able to enforce it—for a while. But don't take it for granted: the most natural reaction is indeed to blame the carrier of bad news.)

6.39111   There is a lot of unacknowledged philosophical significance to the connections between unions and crime. Between legitimized rebellion and the original subversion it issues from. Dialectical processes have their own (revealing!) regressions.

6.3912   Those who protect you from evil are often the carriers of evil. Nowhere do more people get sick than in a hospital. Nowhere do they experience more perversions than in a monastery.

6.392   As any traitor, this one, too, will operate under cover. Dressed up as the enemy. Masquerading as a thing. You will collect all that has been silenced, all those "subjective" activities which resist the real, which involve our being in denial, play, experiment, and make up a substance to be their "subject": make them the activities of a *mind.*

7   "There is" no mind. And yet to claim that there is is to make an important political statement.

7.1   One that ought not, ever, to be "made true"—or its whole point would be lost. It must continue to be uttered foolishly, in defiance of the "facts," straining their "meaning"; it must keep on working as an extraneous body, rejected by the organism, carrying infection, breeding pus. If the mind did indeed become a thing, if "there were" a mind as "there are" tables and chairs, if a final reconciliation between the two were to obtain (the ultimate *Aufhebung*—where the problem, of course, is with "ultimate"), we might as well forget about the mind: the brain would be all we need. (Or we might have an "identity theory" in which the mind *is* the brain, to remind us of what we have lost. We will not regret the loss, if we espouse that theory; but the very redundancy of the theory, the very fact that we have such a useless "tool," will be a signpost for the emotion we are denying.)

7.11   It's highly unlikely that anything can have that kind of permanent destabilizing effect. Each party is in the business of anticipating the opponent's moves and depriving them of effectiveness, and there are few ways of achieving *that* which are as effective as turning surprise into boredom. So pretty soon you will be mumbling "mind is substance" and nothing much will happen: there will no longer be anything "other" to the music of those words, they will no longer be calling anyone to battle. You will have to think of other ways of getting attention. (At some point, in some "sophisticated" circles, you might even be faced by a sort of second-order immunization: by people immunized to *the general practice* of getting attention by dissonant chords. You will say something outrageous and they will appreciate it "aesthetically"—and make you entirely impotent. Then you may have to lie low for a while, or skip town; time must take care of those dodoes before things can start moving again. That's the problem with literature that is too "literary," too "self-conscious"—indeed!) But note that familiar clichés can be revived (history can be a "science," that is, an arena for play). This resurrection can be brought about by making more of the context "speak," by providing more of the articulation that one (usually, and deceptively) feels (is induced to feel) is no longer needed. By going beyond mumbling, into *listening* to what you say—to the coloratura of your piece. Our current practice might have that effect.

7.12   Everything here is a double-edged sword, we know; everything cuts both ways and makes its "owner" bleed. The jargon of transcendentality by which the mind is often honored

is also a defense barrier under which it is hidden and pro-
tected from blows. That defense can be shattered: proved to
be void of "empirical content" (what else would you expect?).
But it can also become *too* successful, stiflingly so. Kant's and
Husserl's transcendental subject is the result of, and is maintained by, a painstaking operation of abstraction. (In Husserl,
the practical, quasi-therapeutic nature of the operation is em-
phasized a good deal more.) This result is constantly at risk
of dissolving when the operation is discontinued, under pressure from ordinary, empirical concerns—those which (for the
moment) cannot be denied, cannot be "played with," which
"it would be a luxury" to play with. The risk will be less, the
less pressing the empirical concerns are. So in the relatively
neutral (relatively luxurious) area of conquered needs (within
middle- to upper-class society) the transcendental subject and
other similar paraphernalia will have a chance of establishing
"firmer" ground. Whence the condescending smile of born-
wealthy intellectuals and their (less fortunate, but ferociously
faithful) butlers (watch out! their time will soon come! they
will inherit the earth, and prove their "essential" loyalty by
duplicating their masters' deeds with a vengeance) when they
point out that, "of course," they are not talking about the
empirical subject. That stability and confidence spell trouble:
they are evidence that the relevant practice is by now *only* disconnected from ordinary ones, and no longer challenges
them—once again, a difference that makes no difference, a
purely exotic, escapist one. Those fighting at the frontier with
the real will derive no comfort or help from such complacency. For complacency *is* their enemy: complacency as such.
It is when the transcendental subject is most in danger, when
it is (felt to be) most threatened, that it can do the most
"good." (To both parties, as usual: a toy revolution may well
be conservatism's best insurance policy. "Enlightened" des-
pots understand that.)

7.2   A whole world of "beliefs," "wishes," "intentions," and the
        like—all *mental* "contents," all "belonging" to that absurd
        structure which the mind is—materializes side by side with
        the public one.

7.21   It claims equal dignity as the public world—as *the world*.

Equal "substance." The *res cogitans* stands proudly next to everything "else." It lumps everything together and confronts it from the outside, claiming it to be only one half, the lesser half, of the story. (This dignity and this pride are what the operation is all about: if you care so much about substantiality—because substantiality defines you—we will take it away from you, and use it to assert its negation. And you will scream, and blame us for contradicting ourselves, and invoke the necessity of a consistent world. You would like that, wouldn't you? The peace of a "sound," well-organized cemetery. But we are not going to be taken in, colonized. This is a two-way street. We will colonize *you*.)

7.211   This presumptuous pronouncement will have more concrete political significance, the less the *res cogitans* is mortified into the conscious, consistent image the public has already imposed on the self—the more the self is able to turn even that image into an excuse for resistance. ("No one quite knows *what* I am. Everyone has a distorted picture of me: I know—I am aware of—that." Though, of course, I am *not* aware of what the right picture is, which should begin to tell me something about picturing and awareness.)

7.22   The mind indeed plays the same game of domination "things" ordinarily play. It tries to master, to incorporate every*thing* (else). To submit it to its logic. To direct its course—to *have directed* its course, whatever that course happened to be.

7.221   Such and such has happened (will happen) because I wanted such and such (and I knew such and such). I intended it to happen. So there is a role for the practical syllogism after all—and one that makes it at least *look* like a good guy. (Though also, generally, a misdirected one. The move it expresses originates in a vindication of the dignity of freedom, but the outcome of that move is often a constraining one. The usual predicament with compromise structures, with pressing something into the service of the opposite party.) And though this character comes fairly late in the day, its point, of course, at the late hour when it comes, is precisely to have always been there, to have been there from the beginning. It is born as an old man, already replete with memories, his life already lived in full. Or it is activated as a prepackaged fantasy: a dream of revolution and terror evoked in all detail by a blow to the neck.

7.2211   I will be the final judge of whether something belongs to me, even if I didn't notice it at the time. If a powerful argument is made that certain projects and goals I was not aware of were part of me, that this hypothesis is the only one that can credibly explain my behavior (and my feelings: pain, fright, anxiety, relief), I will maintain my authority by *re*cognizing those goals and projects (a much better strategy than denying them). In some sense, at some level, I *was* aware of them all along. And, unless I rewrite my history accordingly, unless I consciously endorse it (endorse it to consciousness), no one will be able to "cure" me of my "mental disturbances"— hardly surprising, since those disturbances are your mind at work, doing "its thing," and curing them amounts to handing all control levers to the pod "people."

7.2212   A "problem" surfaces: *bad faith.* How can I possibly lie to myself, make myself not know something—which I must know in order to do anything about it? And how could that possibly work, since I know that I am lying? (You try dividing up "yourself" and it doesn't get you anywhere: one "agency" must still be ruling the field, and must "know what it's doing," know what it is that it doesn't want to know.) My identification with consciousness is carried to paradoxical extremes: if *I* do anything, consciousness does it—or I do it (something in me, the *me* part of me, the one that sides with the public, my *ego*, does it) consciously. Therefore, if I protect myself from public snooping into my subjectivity, *the snooping ends up protecting itself from itself,* and we end up with a big puzzle—which we then try to "resolve." (There must be ways for us to spend our time. Prisoners have a lot of it on their hands, so they make houses with matchsticks, or press wet paper into shapes—sometimes into a gun. None of this is risk-free.) A true case of bad faith if there ever was one. (Though the presence of this "problem" is also a good reminder that even if the self accepts the identification with consciousness, it doesn't really believe it—it is only a strategy, a ploy.)

7.2213 Let "us" recapitulate, and insist on distinctions that define this story—and its politics. To begin with, there is subjectivity, that is, diversity, dialogue, confrontation, multiplicity of patterns, manifold. Not a peaceful, relaxed confrontation, but one in which every party uses all the strength it has available to impose itself on the others, to cancel them, to be more conspicuous than they are. Then there surface (at least) three other matters: privacy (the disconnecting, isolating of subjectivity as a means of defending established structures from its potential violence), consciousness (a prying, malevolent eye that exposes some of the workings of subjectivity, denies some others, and in general tries to fashion—to tie up—subjectivity into a coherent story, into a secondary elaboration that is now supposed to be living "my" life), and mind (the impertinent erection of subjectivity into an object of overwhelming importance, on a par with all that is not mind—which is to say, with all that is). Each of these matters can serve opposite interests, even at the same time: can be a tool of revolution or tyranny, or (most likely) both. Specific situations will have to be studied one at a time, to bring out the specific balance of forces each of them instantiates. But you want to be clear concerning how the various tools function, and how *differently* they can (each) function. Then you will see that, say, the consistent story into which "my" consciousness is trying to lock me (that is, lock the subject I am) can be used to confer credibility on the provocative, irritating claim that I—the very negation of objects, of objectivity—am an object, so that the claim might continue to exercise its provocation a while longer, might buy time for its terrorist activity. Or, conversely, that that same story can be turned to making "room" for me in a world of objects, to making me perfectly comfortable with an objective, thinglike view of myself: I am such and such, I can expect such and such from myself, if you press such and such a button in me you will have such and such a response. *And* you will see the strategic significance of talking casually, matter-of-factly, about "my conscious mind," as if "my," "conscious," and "mind" belonged to a single (complex, but still original—and originally integrated) reality: you will see that phrase (and the identity it intimates, with deceptive naturalness) as a weapon (of disinformation, of propaganda), though in the abstract you won't be able to determine whose weapon it is.

7.2214   There are those who are obsessed with accounting for the unity of a form of life—specifically, "our" own. They are not satisfied with bringing out various aspects of it; they need to know (to tell) how these are all aspects of one and the same thing. Here the emphasis is quite different. There is unity in the narrative sense: you can understand how those various aspects came to be, how indeed they had to. But, synchronically, the landscape we depicted is dominated by *dis*organization and disconnectedness. Adapting a metaphor by Freud, we can think of this landscape as an ancient town: all its buildings were built for a reason, but as you now look at them next to one another, you are struck by how much they do *not* belong together. Or, better, you ought to be so struck; it is part of the point of this narrative to make you so struck. For you are, of course, familiar with that mess, and familiar things no longer look strange—however strange they might *be.* You walk down via dei Fori Imperiali toward piazza Venezia and see the Colosseum and the Fori next to a baroque church next to Mussolini's Altare della Patria next to Palazzo Venezia next to the Campidoglio, and everything seems to be exactly right. You sense a peculiar, perverse harmony. (How often did I find that I had gotten used to something that just wasn't supposed to be where it was—except that I could no longer *see* that!)

7.222   On a larger scale, everything has happened (will happen) because someone like myself (only much more powerful, infinitely more powerful) intended it, because of what she wanted (and knew). Of what she has *always* wanted, before time even existed.

7.2221   Religion again, this time with a more cordial, motherly appearance (well attuned to the Christian way station). Religion as prudence, as careful planning for a better future, as providential economy. God as someone to trust, to whom to trust oneself. Except that, to maintain consistency with the previous "incarnation" (consistency is what this party is all about—it has consistent interests to defend, the interests of consistency), the plan here must be a secret, mysterious, incomprehensible one. You must believe it to be for the best, but it's not up to you to determine what "best" is. ("Is something good because God wants it, or does God want it because it is good?" The old question surfaces again, and again it will not be answered. Because no one really *cares* for an answer.) You have trusted yourself blindly, put all your resources into a blind trust, and don't even have an independent notion (independent, that is, of whoever administers the trust) of what a "good use" of those resources would be.

7.2222   But, of course, this mystery is a pretense, a smoke screen. As you find yourself streamlined into compliance by the ritual, as you experience in it the most repetitive, numbing exteriority, as you are told to do thing after dopey thing "just because," you can always think of it all (the mystery makes it possible for you to think of it all) as perpetrating some ultimate, triumphant liberation. You see conformism rule, you see those who believe the rhetoric, and have it spread into action, ousted and abused by the hierarchy, you see the hierarchy clearly aligned with the most despicable status quo; but the alibi is always available that someone else knows better, and you don't, so you should just obey. (Blind obedience will get you to heaven, when nothing matters anymore.) The respect for that difference which is constitutive of you has become a purely formal structure (mysterious Other = Other as a form without content, a form that cannot be articulated), which empowers an entirely opposite, inimical practice (not necessarily inimical to you—to the empirical you—but inimical to difference).

7.2223   And yet the very existence of the mystery might work as an invitation to playfully unravel it. Knowing full well that no resolution is possible (it is not going to be allowed), but precisely for that reason reassured that such playing is harmless—and therefore encouraged to continue in it.

7.23   Some will protest loudly against this subordination of the real.

7.231   They will claim that there is only the real, and all that other stuff is a myth, remnants of an older, more primitive era. Fuzzy, cozy, pathetic folklore. Which doesn't even deserve to

be "translated" into a new, more respectable jargon, reconstructed within a "scientific" framework, identified with "objective" structures; which must simply be junked, eliminated
without residue, without mercy. They don't care for archaeol-
ogy; they want to bring the bulldozers out and level the
ground.

7.232   We know that they are right, that what they say is true (that
it is *truth itself*), and we also know that we ought to resist
it—resist its gaining currency, its becoming the basis for (political, repressive) action (that this resistance is *"ought to"* it-
self: ethical precisely because it is impossible). We know that
indeed "there is" only the real, as a result of a forceful selection and a bloody struggle. And we also know that we should
not forget what "there isn't," what has been forced into a position of falsity, what didn't make it through but still vies for
attention, condemns the essential injustice of the "ontology."
Speaks from nowhere, without a leg to stand on, in the name
of nothing. That is, in the name of freedom, of subjectivity.
Of the most tantalizing of questions: Why not?

7.233   Purifying our language of all references to that mythological
stuff is one more attempt at neutering it, *and* at neutering the
nonbeing for which language is the best chance. At conjuring
a structure that is language's kiss of death: "the language of
total administration."

7.2331   Bureaucrats move their tongues and emit sounds; they scratch
paper with their pens; they move their fingers on computer
keys. But they are silent; language never enters their lives.
What is not is never there, in the *stories* that they are, that
make them bureaucrats. (And their silence—the music of it—
is quite helpful in maintaining the hold of those stories, in
reinforcing their nature as bureaucrats.)

7.2332   Which allows us to come to terms with an age-old perplexity:
How come we don't call what the wind does to the desert
sand "writing," though it might be indistinguishable from
what someone would write? We can see this now as a clever
question: one that cleverly (perhaps too much so, for its own
good) smuggles in the very issue of contention—and then

finds itself in the presence of a contentious issue. For "indistinguishable" clearly means here: having exactly the same existing, apparent traits. Where the difference, of course, is made precisely by what does not exist and cannot appear. By the role assigned in the story accounting for a language *being* a language to what does not exist and cannot appear. (And remember: there may well be a story about the wind and the sand that makes the wind's a language. It is implicitly assumed in the example that there isn't—the story of the example is told in such a way as to suggest that implication.)

7.23321   So, ultimately, I side with the analysis that makes the wind's not a language because it does not express *intentional* behavior. But I can only side with it now, after exploding its deceptively "pat" character, after bringing out the struggles it glosses over. And after showing that saying just that (the wind's behavior is not intentional) is not yet an analysis, but only the promise of one—that it still has a lot of work ahead of itself.

7.234   Though—who knows?—this neutering process might even be "for the best." Folk psychology is, after all, the compromise outcome of an earlier, less thorough (and maybe, for that reason, more effective?) attempt to control subjectivity; so debunking it might result not in wiping out the latter but, on the contrary, in letting it loose, out of control. No longer watched, no longer claimed to be existent—and hence freer. Better able to chip away at what is existent, and eventually crack it, because able to do so invisibly. (What you don't know about, what you can't see, can hurt you the most.)

7.235   Would *I* like that development? Probably not: I want to continue to make subjectivity subservient to *my* ends. *I* as this body of "mine," this pile of cells and tics, this desperately defensive structure. *I* as this particular story, which is one of many, of infinitely many—a story that the subject will soon laugh at, that indeed it is already laughing at, though that laughter has not yet (perhaps) made it to "reality," it is still only heard in the back room, is still not resonating in the halls, much like a *silent,* scornful grin. And I know all of that,

and in the most basic sense I don't care—that very not caring
is what I am, is *that* I am. I am because I hold on to myself,
without a reason, without feeling that I need a reason.

7.236   And this, of course, contradicts pretty much everything I said.

7.2361 Not so much for the constant emphasis on multiplicity, which
is denied by this arrogant assertion of (personal) identity. I
have left enough traces behind to provide a justification for
that contradiction. I have been presenting my theory as a general one, within which room must—and can—be found
for the very operation of presenting it: for the partial, biased
point of view from which it is presented.

7.2362 The real problem is the tone of the assertion: its arrogance,
that is. All along, (infinite) articulation has been treated with
the greatest favor, assigned the highest value. Beginnings,
foundations, intuitions have been looked at as just limitations, weaknesses. As nothing to be proud of: an indication
that our time and energy are finite, and hence some things
we will have no time or energy to call in question. So the present assertion of an unquestioned stand should be uttered in
shame; there should be a furtive, guilty look that goes with it.
And, what counts even more, the same embarrassed attitude
should accompany the statement of the theory itself, which is,
again, one of many, proposed for no reason. But there is none
of that (though there is talk of it): this theory of dislocation
and playfulness and nonbeing is phrased just as confidently as
any traditional theory—any theory espousing the practical
syllogism and providing "rational" recipes for success. There
are ways in which one could try to reconcile oneself with this
feature. One could play the deconstructive, Hegelian game
that "seriousness" can only be subverted from the inside.
Or one could say, "What would you expect? This pragmatic
conflict *shows,* better than anything the theory could *say,* its
rejection of the practical syllogism—of the ideal of exercising
theoretical control over action. You say something, and the
very act of saying it contradicts it; so your saying *in fact* does
not control your acting." Still, no such "rationalization" de-
tracts from how odd it feels that I should be speaking as I am,
given what I am saying. Which, *the theory would say,* is ex-

actly as it should be: if it weren't odd, it wouldn't matter—
there would be no point to saying it. It matters because it feels
odd, it feels as if it can't quite be said. In the theory, this is a
perfectly general conclusion.

8   Only what we cannot speak about must we not pass over in
         silence.

Designer:	U.C. Press Staff
Compositor:	J. Jarrett Engineering, Inc.
Text:	10/13 Sabon
Display:	Sabon
Printer & Binder:	Thomson Shore